C000229483

STOKE·ON·TRENT

ESTATE PUBLICATIONS
Bridewell House,
Tenterden, Kent.
Tel. 05806 4225

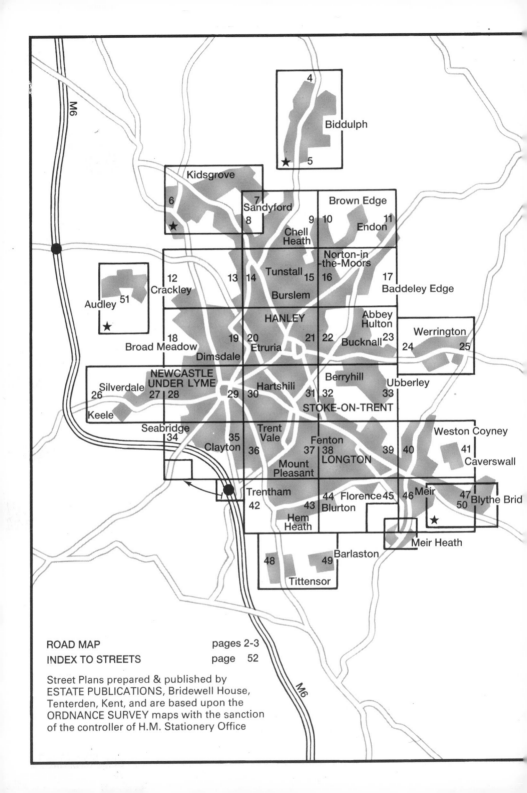

M6

4
Biddulph
5

Kidsgrove

6

7
Sandyford
8

Brown Edge
9 10   11
                Endon
Chell
Heath

12   13 14 Tunstall 15 Norton-in
Crackley   -the-Moors
                                 16
Audley 51   17
                     Burslem   Baddeley Edge

HANLEY   Abbey
                         Hulton
18   19 20   21 22   23 Werrington
Broad Meadow Etruria   Bucknall 24   25
         Dimsdale

NEWCASTLE   Berryhill
UNDER LYME   Ubberley
Silverdale   Hartshill
26   27 28   29 30 31 32 33
Keele   STOKE-ON-TRENT

Seabridge   Trent   Weston Coyney
34   35 Vale Fenton   39 40   41
Clayton 36   37 38   Caverswall
              Mount LONGTON
              Pleasant   47
Trentham   Florence   50 Blythe Brid
42   43 44   45 46 Meir
         Hem Blurton
         Heath   Meir Heath

48   49 Barlaston
         Tittensor

ROAD MAP   pages 2-3
INDEX TO STREETS   page   52

Street Plans prepared & published by
ESTATE PUBLICATIONS, Bridewell House,
Tenterden, Kent, and are based upon the
ORDNANCE SURVEY maps with the sanction
of the controller of H.M. Stationery Office

ESTATE PUBLICATIONS

STOKE·ON·TRENT

NEWCASTLE·UNDER·LYME

AUDLEY · BIDDULPH
BLYTHE BRIDGE · KIDSGROVE

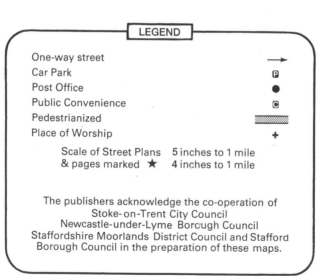

LEGEND

One-way street	→
Car Park	P
Post Office	●
Public Convenience	C
Pedestrianized	▨
Place of Worship	✛

Scale of Street Plans   5 inches to 1 mile
& pages marked ★   4 inches to 1 mile

The publishers acknowledge the co-operation of
Stoke-on-Trent City Council
Newcastle-under-Lyme Borough Council
Staffordshire Moorlands District Council and Stafford
Borough Council in the preparation of these maps.

Estate Publications 230B   0 86084 367 X   Crown Copyright reserved

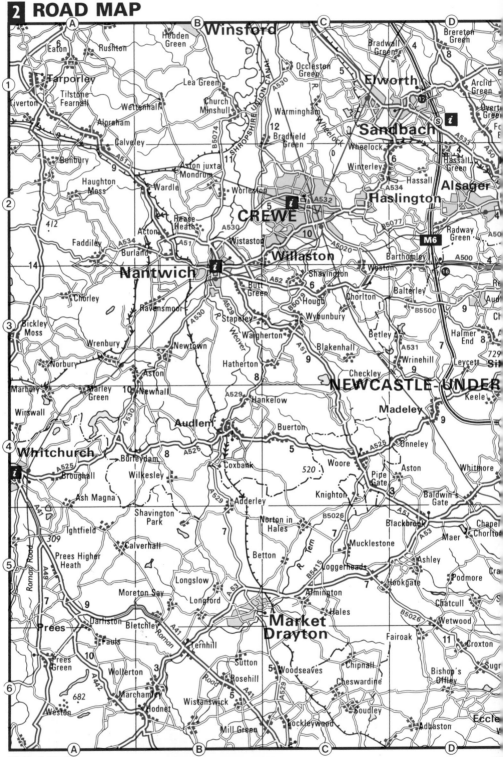

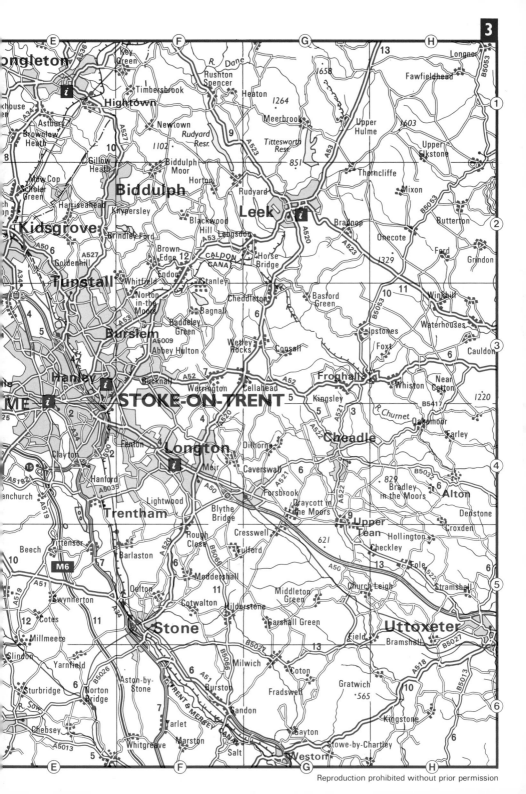

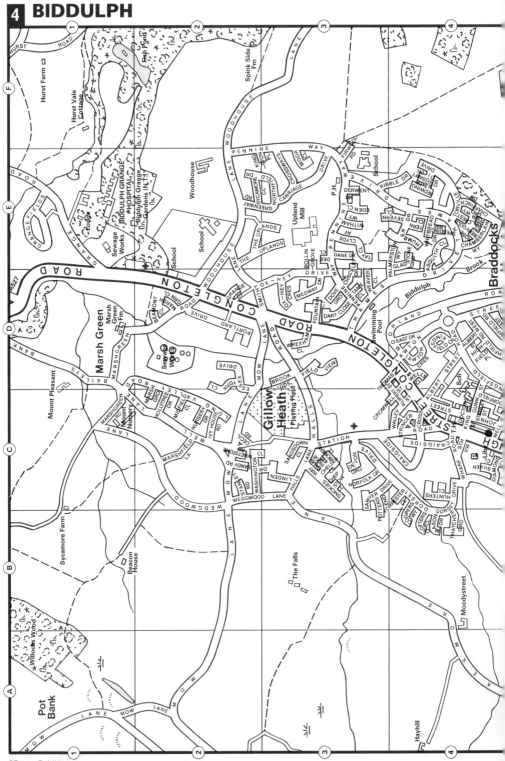

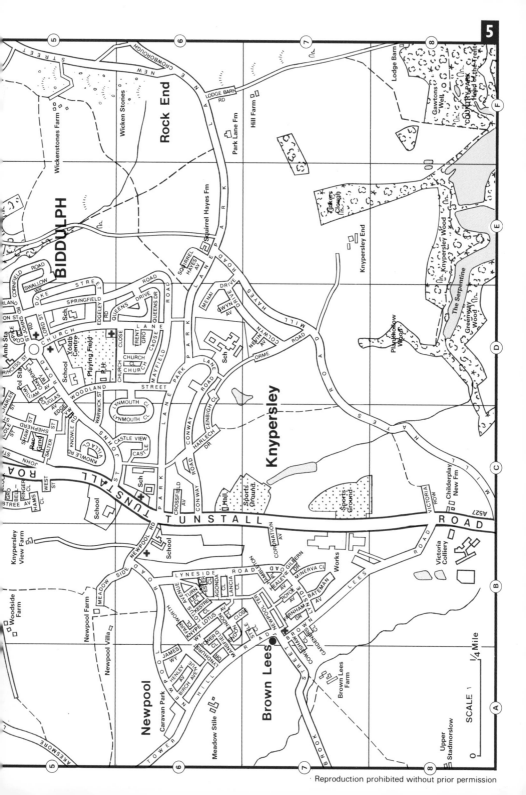

5

SCALE $\frac{1}{4}$ Mile

Reproduction prohibited without prior permission

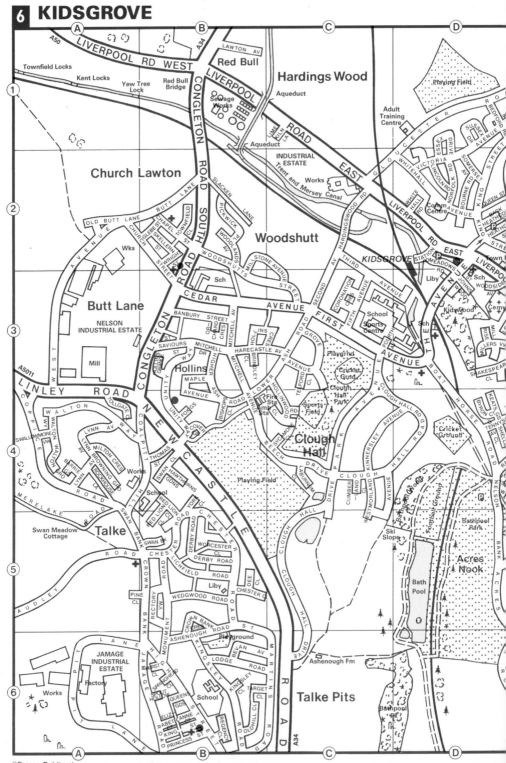

6 KIDSGROVE

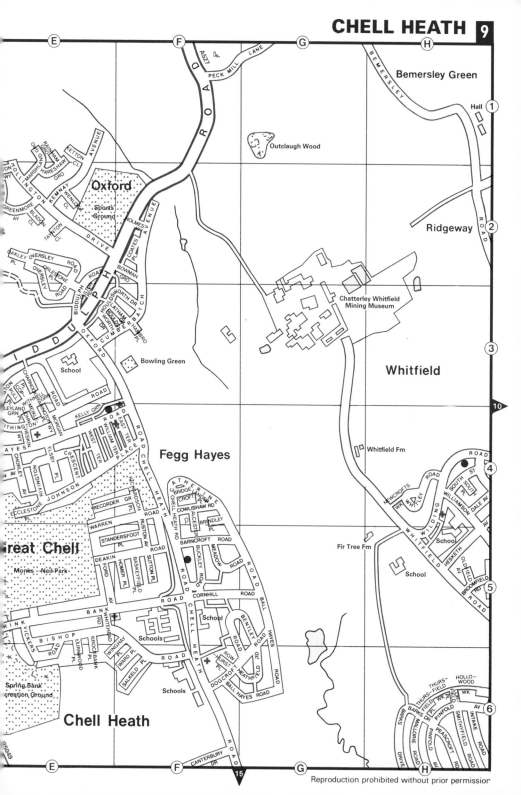

E F G H

PECK MILL LANE
A527
A527 ROAD

BEMERSLEY

Bemersley Green

Hall 1

Outclaugh Wood

Ridgeway 2

Oxford

Sports Ground

Chatterley Whitfield Mining Museum

3

Whitfield

10

Bowling Green

School

Whitfield Fm

ROAD 4

SOUTH ST
SOUTH ST
WILLIAMSON
DALE AV

KELLY GRN
EAST TER
WILLIAM TER
WEST TER

Fegg Hayes

CHORLEY
JOHNSON

ECCLESTONE PL

BRIDGE
CROFT
COWLISHAW RD
ALCESTER
BRINDLEY PL

Fir Tree Fm

School

WKLEY
WHITFIELD
NEWCROFTS
ROAD
WILDING ROAD
HESKETH
OLDFIELD

School 5
BROOMFIELD RD

reat Chell

Monks - Neil Park

RECORDER GR
RICHARDSON PL
WARREN
STANDERSFOOT
RUSTON AV
BARNCROFT ROAD
MEADOW ROAD
ROAD
ROAD

DEAKIN
FORD
HOMER PL
BASKEYFIELD PL
SUTTON PL
BUCKLEY ROAD

CORNHILL ROAD
BALL
HAYES

BANK RD
VICKERS
BISHOP
BARNWOOD PL
BROCKBANK PL
WINGWAY PL
WARD PL
SALKELD PL

School
Schools

BENTLEY RD
ROAD

Spring Bank creation Ground

Schools

ROW
DOGCROFT RD
HEATH RD
BALL HAYES ROAD
OLD

Chell Heath

HOLLO-WOOD
THURS-FIELD
BARKS FIELD PL
WK
WK
AV 6
BARNS DRIVE
MALLORIE ROAD
PINFOLD
PINFOLD AV
PEASCROFT RD
SMITHFIELD ROAD
INTAKE ROAD

E F G H
CANTERBURY DR

15

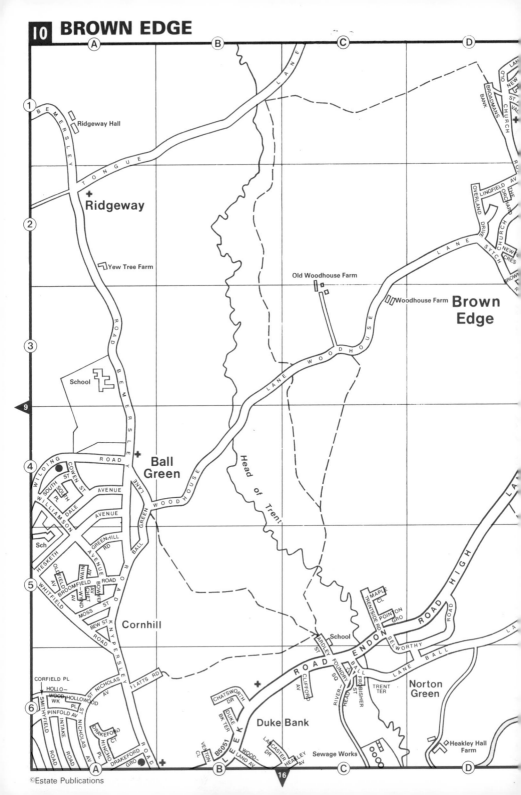

A   B   C   D

Ridgeway Hall

1

BEMERSLEY

TONGUE LANE

Ridgeway

2

Yew Tree Farm

Old Woodhouse Farm

Woodhouse Farm

Brown Edge

BROADMANS BANK

OLD NEW VAL ST LANE

CHURCH RD

LINGFIELD ORCHARD AV

OVERLAND DRIVE

CHURCH SYCH

NEW CRES

BROWN R

3

School

BEMERSLEY ROAD

WOODHOUSE LANE

9

Ball Green

WILDING

COWEN ST

SOUTH DALE

SOUTH ST

AVENUE

WILLIAMSON

AVENUE

4

Sch

HESKETH

GREEN HILL RD

OLDFIELD WYND

NEWMAN AV

CHET

BROOMFIELD AV

WHITFIELD

MOSS ST

BEW ST

BALL GREEN ROAD

WOODHOUSE LANE

KNYPERSLEY ROAD

Head of Trent

MAPLE CL

TRENTSIDE RD

POINTON GRO

School

HARDLEY ST

FOUNDRY SQ

RIVER-HEAD

FROBISHER ST

BALL ST

SEWORTHY

TRENT TER

ENDON ROAD

HIGH ROAD

BALL LANE

LANE

Norton Green

5

Cornhill

ROAD

CORFIELD PL

HOLLO- WOOD WK

HOLLOWOOD PL

SMITHFIELD

NICHOLAS AV

ILATTS RD

CHATSWORTH DR

CLIFFORD AV

6

PINFOLD AV

INTAKE

DRAKEFORD CT

HINCHO

NICHOLAS AV

DRAKEFORD GRO

BK TER

DUKE ST

VERNON CL

B5051

LANCASTER DR

WOOD- LAND AV

HEAKLEY AV

Duke Bank

Sewage Works

BLEEK ROAD

Heakley Hall Farm

A   B   16   C   D

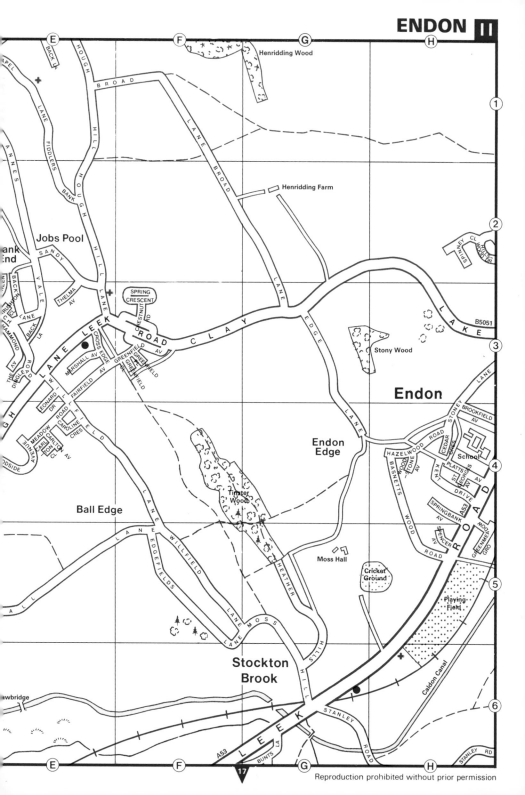

Henridding Wood

Henridding Farm

Jobs Pool

SPRING CRESCENT

Stony Wood

Endon

Endon Edge

Timster Wood

Ball Edge

Moss Hall

Cricket Ground

School

Playing Field

Caldon Canal

Stockton Brook

awbridge

B5051

SPINNEY CL

HOUGH HILL

BROAD LANE

CLAY

LAKE LANE

EDGE LANE

LEEK ROAD

STONEY ROAD

CEDAR AV

HAZELWOOD AV

BASNETTS WOOD ROAD

SPRINGBANK AV

SPENCER AV

GREENMEAD GRO

WILLFIELD LANE

EDGEFIELDS LANE

HEATHER

MOSS HILLS

STANLEY

BUNTS LA

A53

STANLEY RD

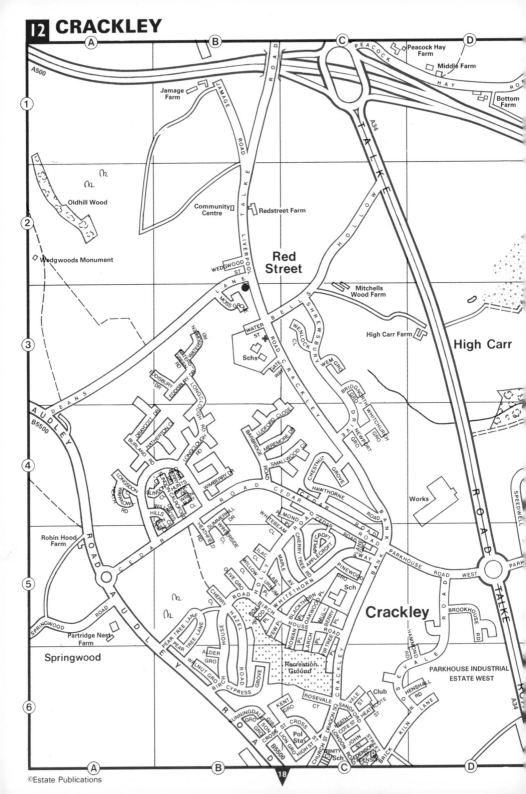

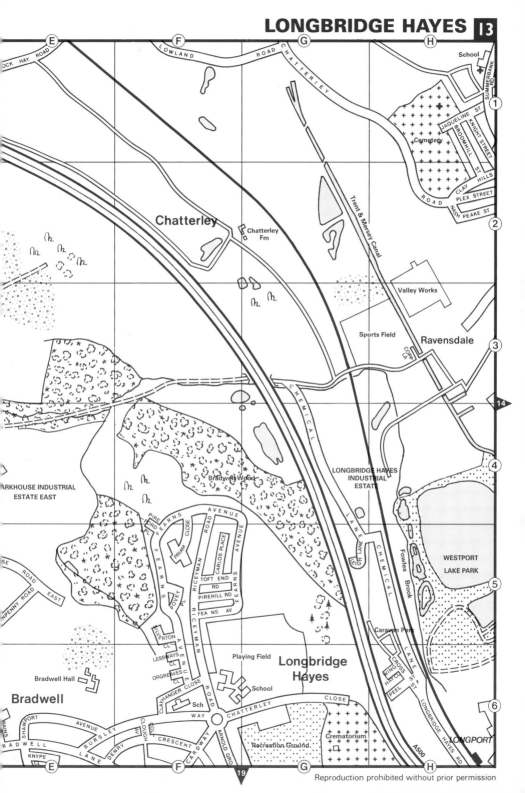

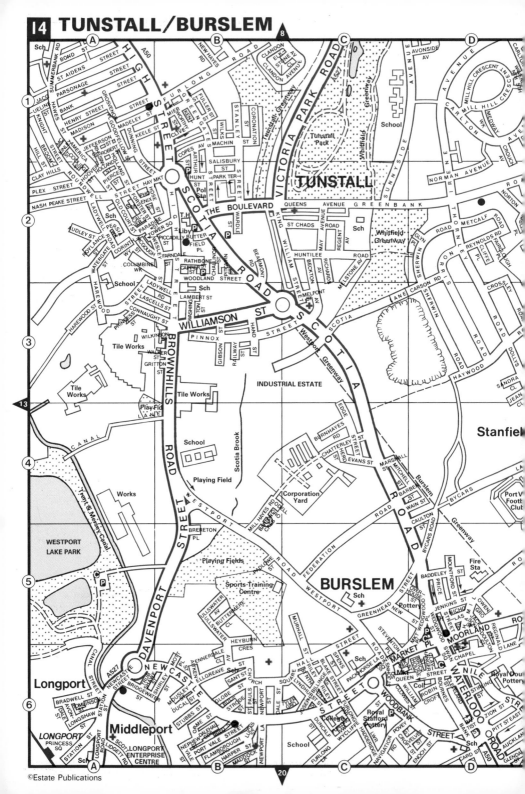

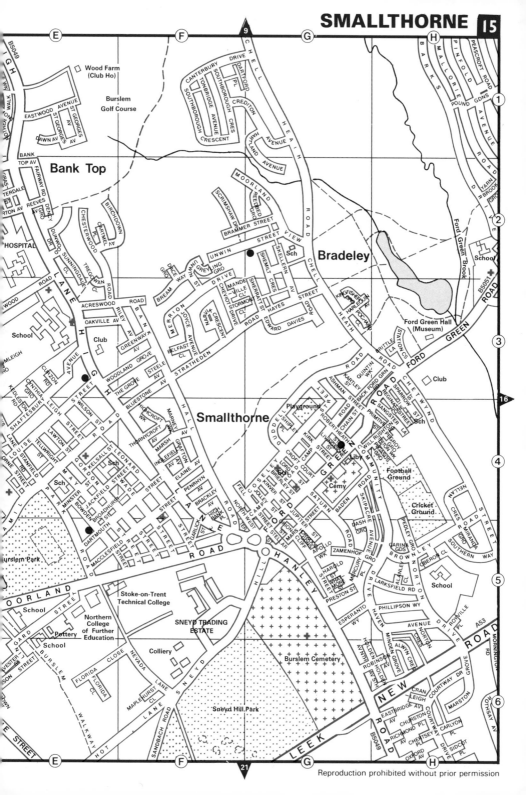

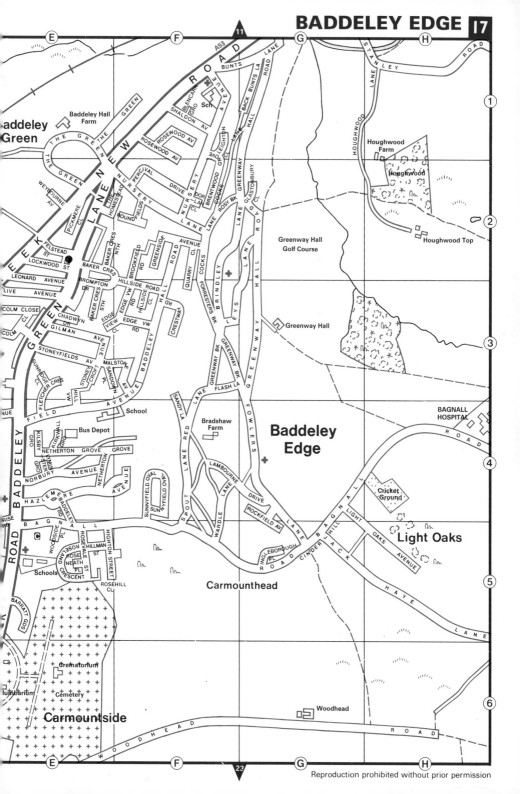

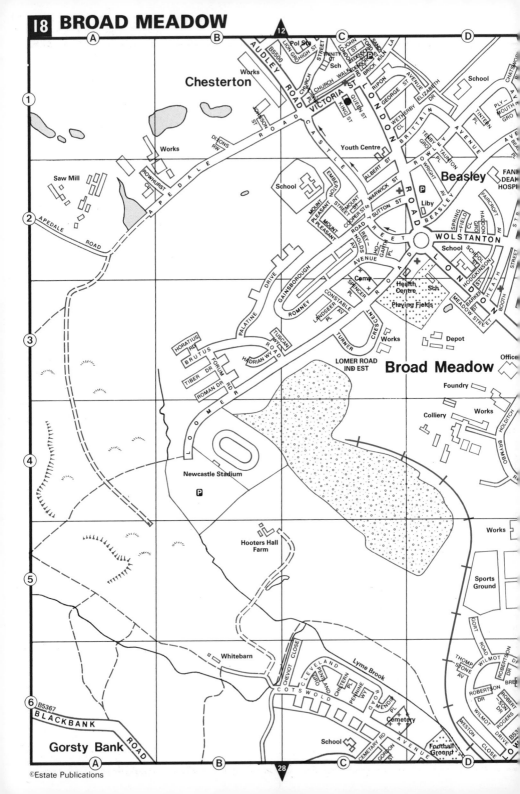

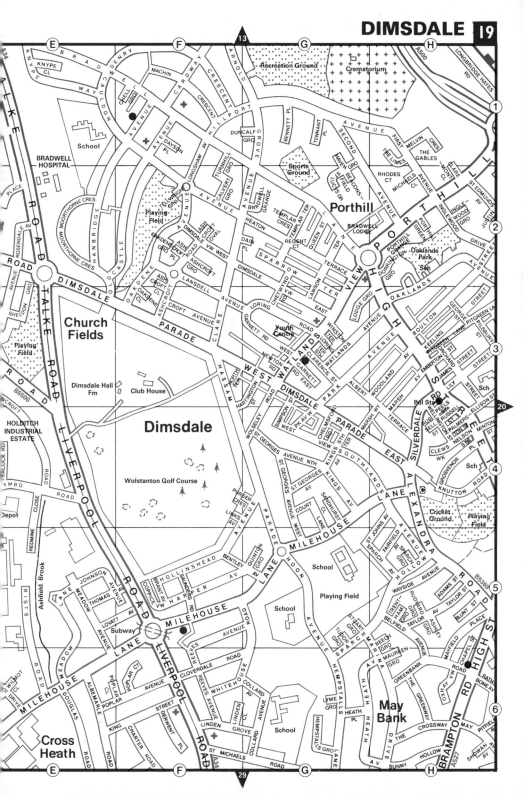

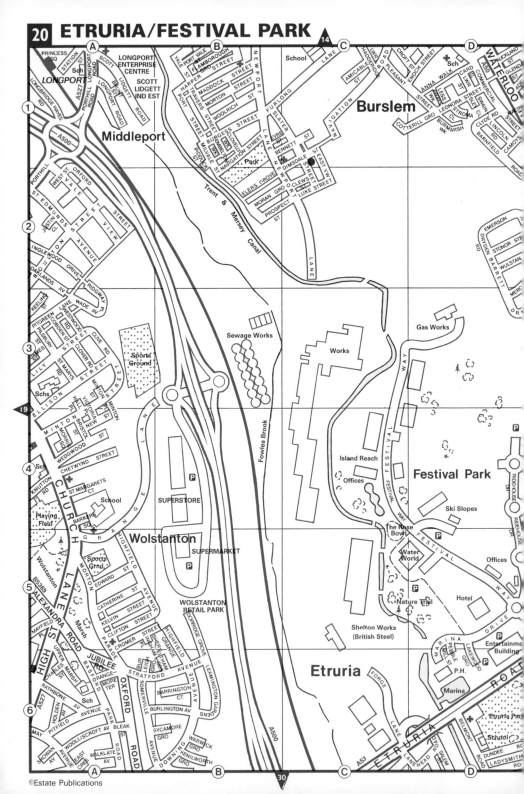

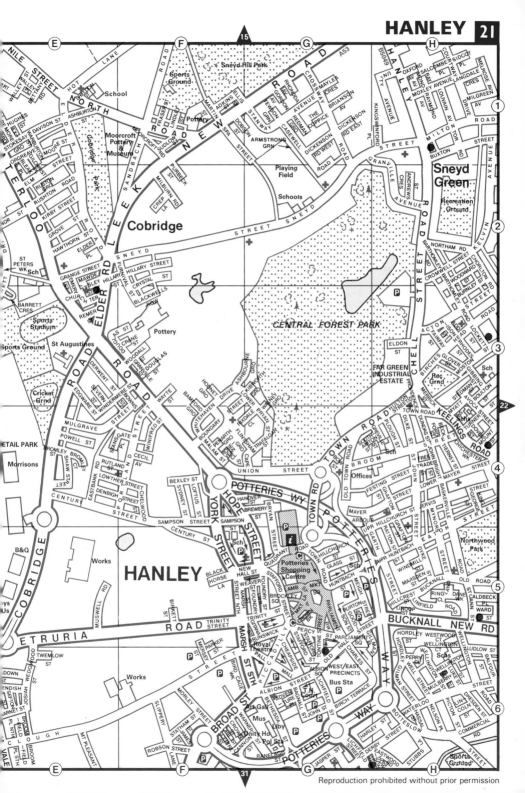

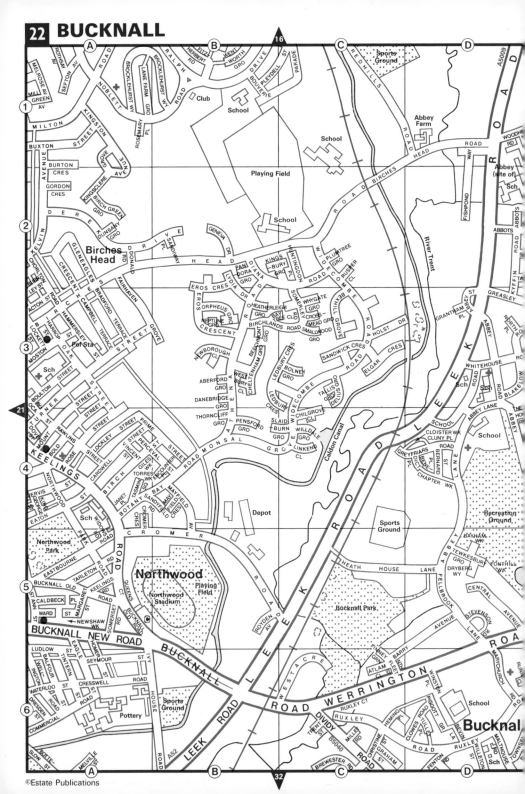

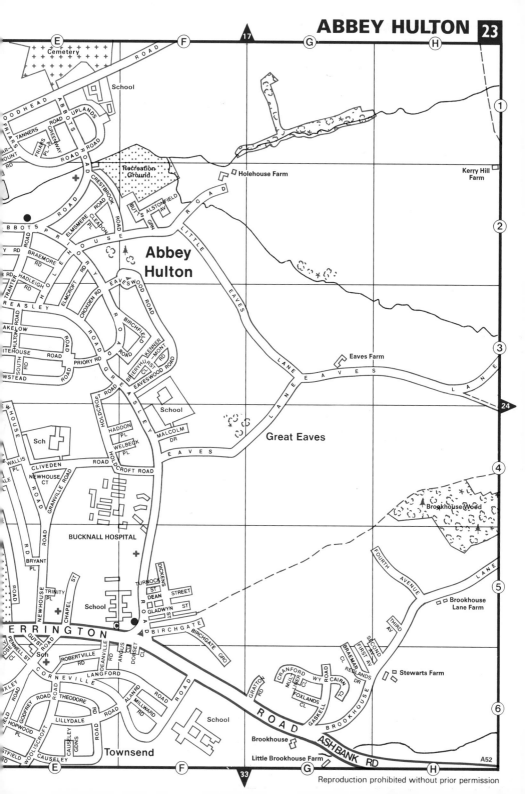

E Cemetery F 17 G H

ROAD

1

OODHEAD

FRIARS
MOUNT
RD

TANNERS

ABBOTS GREENWAY

UPLANDS ROAD

FRIAR ST

School

ABBOTS ROAD

CHESTBROOK

HOUSE ROAD

Recreation Ground

ALSTONFIELD AV

BUTS GRN

Holehouse Farm

Kerry Hill Farm

2

BBOTS ROAD

Y RD

BRAEMORE RD

TRANTER

HADLEIGH RD

REASLEY

ELMSMERE

ELMCROFT RD

CLEADON PL

PRIORY

HOUSE ROAD

CROXDEN RD

Abbey Hulton

EAVESWOOD ROAD

LITTLE EAVES

ROAD

AKELOW

ITEHOUSE ROAD

SOUTH HULTON ROAD

WSTEAD

PRIORY RD

ROYAL ROAD

BIRCHFIELD

BITTERWURST CL

KENNER ST

EAVESWOOD ROAD

MONT

Eaves Farm

LANE EAVES

3

HOLDCROFT ROAD

REASLEY

School

MALCOLM DR

Great Eaves

EAVES

LANE

EAVES

LANE

24

HOUSE ROAD

WALLIS PL

Sch

HADDON PL

WELBECK PL

CLIVEDEN

HOLDCROFT ROAD

Brookhouse Wood

4

NEWHOUSE CT

GRANVILLE ROAD

ROAD

BUCKNALL HOSPITAL

FOURTH AVENUE

LANE

5

RD

BRYANT PL

NEWHOUSE PL

TRINITY PL

CHAPEL ST

ST

School

DICKENS ST

TURNOCK ST

DEAN STREET

GLADWYN ST

ROAD

THIRD AV

SECOND AV

FIRST AV

BRAEMAR DR

Brookhouse Lane Farm

Stewarts Farm

ERRINGTON

C

BIRCHGATE

BIRCHGATE GRO

ROBERTVILLE RD

GUYS ST

PENNELL ST

ROAD

Sch

CORNEVILLE

DEANVILLE RD

ANGUS ST

DORSET CL

LANGFORD ROAD

REDLANDS DR

CRANFORD CL

MULLINER WY

FOXLANDS CL

GASKELL

CAIRN

ROAD

GRATTON RD

BROOKHOUSE

6

XLEY

HOPWOOD PL

GODFREY ROAD

THEODORE ROAD

WOOLISCROFT RD

CAUSELEY GDNS

LILLYDALE

ALLARD RD

MILLWARD RD

ROAD

ROAD

School

ROAD

ASHBANK RD

Brookhouse

Little Brookhouse Farm

Townsend

STFIELD

CAUSELEY

E F 33 G H

A52

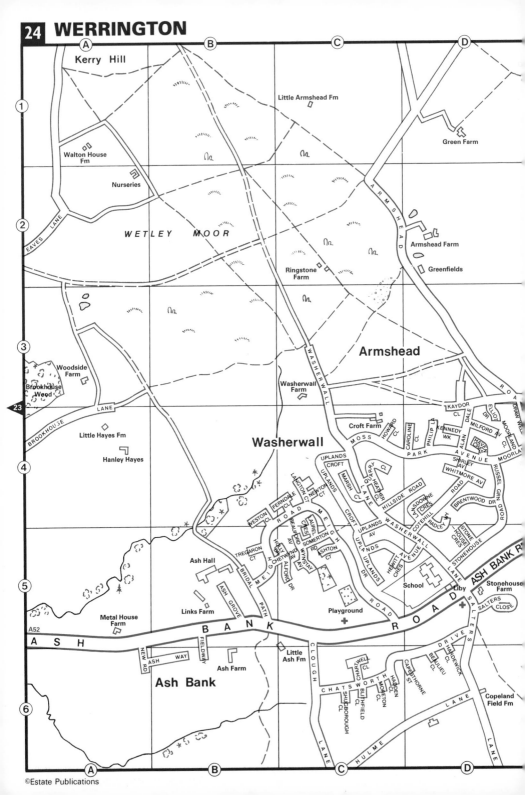

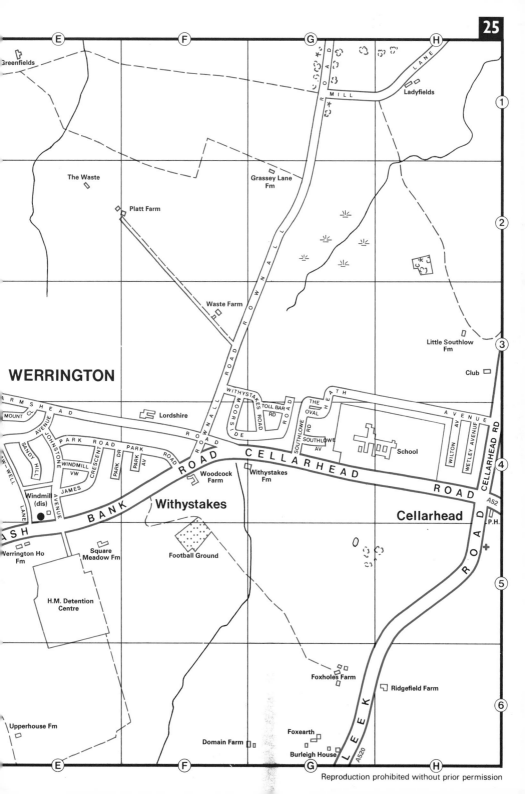

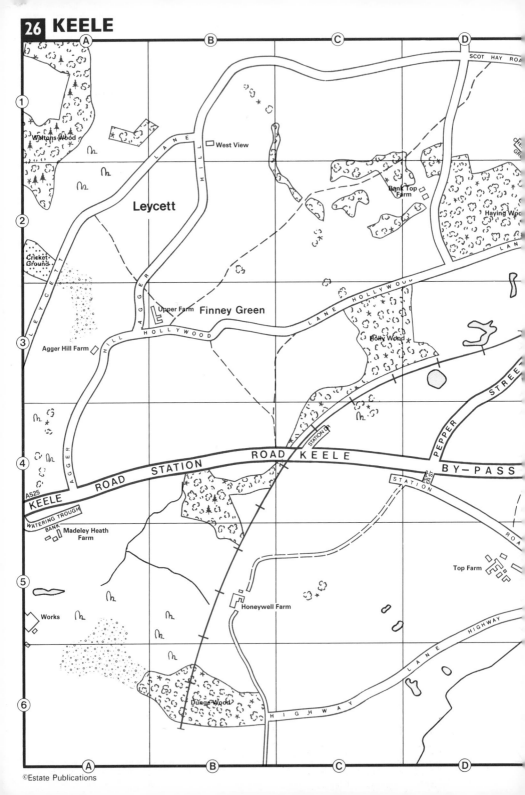

A   B   C   D

1

Waltons Wood

West View

Leycett

2

Cricket Ground

Bank Top Farm

Haying Wood

SCOT HAY ROAD

Upper Farm   Finney Green

HOLLYWOOD

HOLLYWOOD LANE

Agger Hill Farm

HILL

AGGER

LANE

HIGH LANE

LEYCETT

3

Holly Wood

PEPPER STREET

4

KEELE   ROAD   STATION   ROAD   KEELE   BY-PASS

A525

AGGER

STATION

STATION

HIGH ST

ROAD

Top Farm

WATERING TROUGH

BANK

Madeley Heath Farm

5

Works

Honeywell Farm

HIGHWAY LANE

6

Dunge Wood

HIGHWAY

A   B   C   D

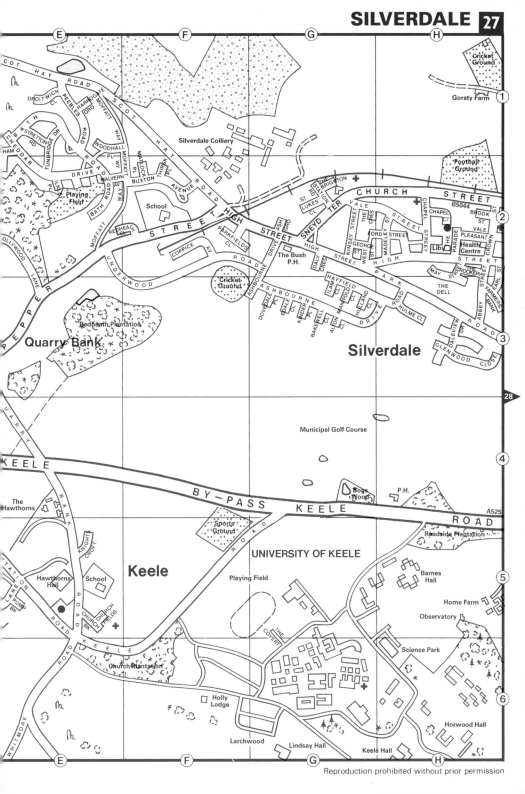

E F G H

1

Cricket Ground

Gorsty Farm

COT HAY ROAD
DROITWICH CL
PEEBLES
HARROGATE
MOFFATT
GRO
SCOT
HAY
ROAD
Silverdale Colliery

Football Ground

BATH
CHEDDAR
RD
STRETTONE DR
TUNBRIDGE DR
HAM
WOODHALL
MOFFATT
WAY
ILK
MALVERN
AV
BUXTON
THIRLK
AVENUE
MATLOCK
DRIVE
PL
BATH ROAD
REDHEATH PL
School
STREET
HIGH
STREET

2

THE STATION
BRIGHTON
ST
CHURCH STREET
STREET
CHAPEL
CHAPEL CT
B5044
BROOK ST
VALE
PLEASANT
ST
CROWN
Libv
THE PARADE
Health Centre
STREET
FARMERS BANK
EARL ST

3

MOFFATT
PL
HOLLYWOOD LANE
Playing Field
UNDERWOOD
ROAD
COPPICE
AV
PARKFIELDS
CL
ASH
GRO
SNEYD
TER
HIGH
CRES
DALY
CRES
GEORGE
ST
KINSEY STREET
WEST ST
MADELY ST
FORD ST
STREET
HIGH
STREET
MAY ST
SYLVESTER STREET
THE ROOKERY
THE DELL
Cricket Ground
The Bush P.H.
ASHBOURNE DRIVE CL
ASHBOURNE PL
DOVEDALE PL
EDALE PL
KINDER PL
BAKEWELL
ALTON
MANIFOLD
HILLIAND
HILLTOP
HAYFIELD CL
PARK
DRIVE
HULME CL
HULME
ROAD
DALEVIEW
DRT
ABBEY ROAD
GLENWOOD CLOSE

PEPPER RD

Quarry Bank

Redheath Plantation

Silverdale

28

4

Municipal Golf Course

KEELE BY-PASS
KEELE ROAD A525
QUARRY BANK
K E E L E

The Hawthorns

Bogs Wood
P.H.
Roadside Plantation

Sports Ground

5

UNIVERSITY OF KEELE

Keele

Hawthorns Hall
School
KNIGHTS CROFT
CHURCH FIELDS
KEELE ROAD
STATION LANE
PUMP BK

Playing Field

THE COVERT

Barnes Hall
Home Farm
Observatory
Science Park

6

Church Plantation

Holly Lodge

Larchwood
Lindsay Hall
Keele Hall

Horwood Hall

WHITMORE

E F G H

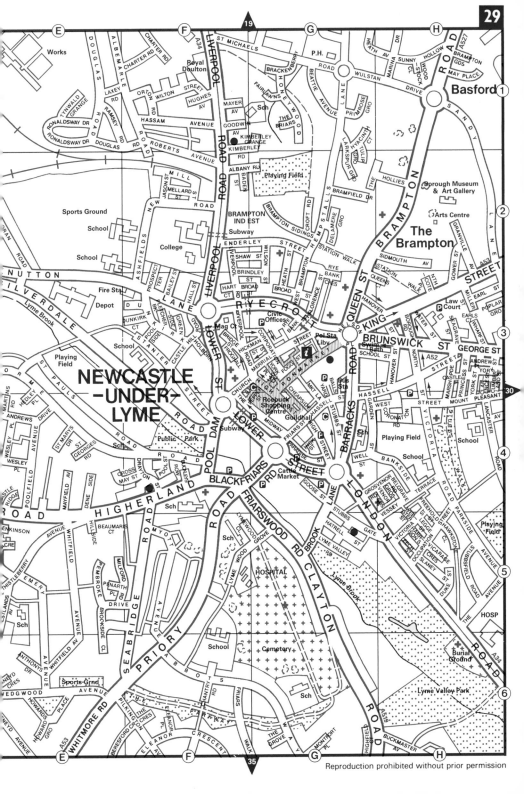

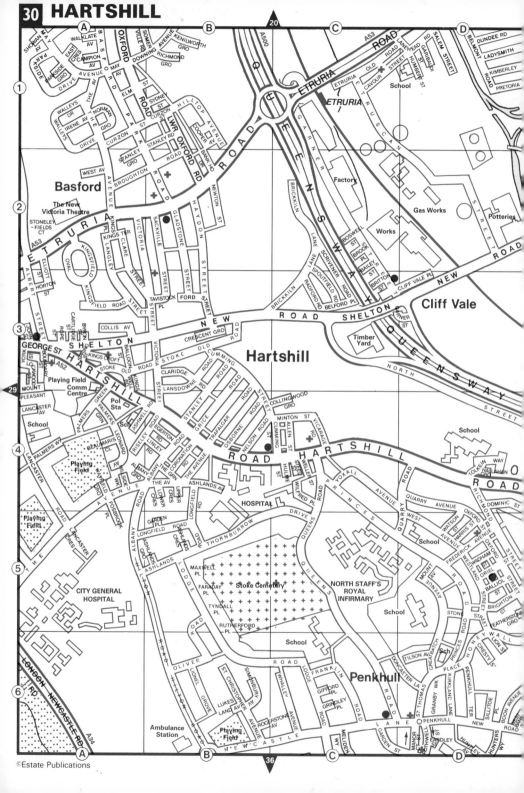

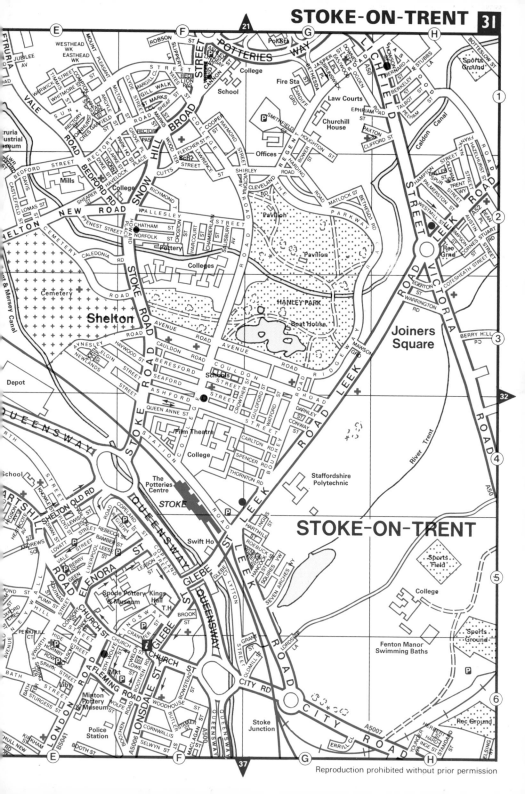

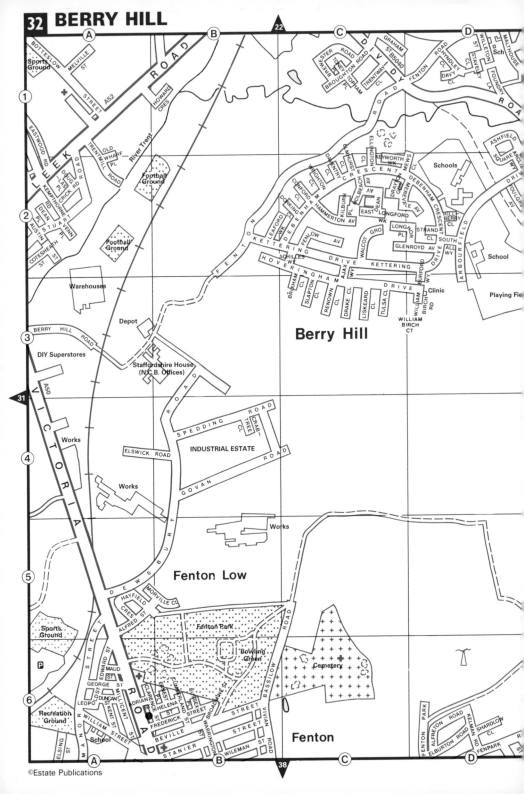

A   B   22   C   D

Sports Ground

MELVILLE ST

HOWARD CRES

BOTTESLOW

STREET

EASTWOOD RD

TRENTMILL ROAD

OLD WHARF PL

River Trent

A52

CREEK

KEMPTHORNE RD

CRICK RD

DRUG RD

DEAN PL

AUSTIN ST

STUART RD

YENN

COTESHEATH ST

Football Ground

Football Ground

Warehouses

Depot

BERRY HILL ROAD

DIY Superstores

VICTORIA

A50

Staffordshire House
(N.C.B. Offices)

Works

ELSWICK ROAD

Works

INDUSTRIAL ESTATE

SPEDDING ROAD

CRAB TREE CL

GOVAN ROAD

Works

Fenton Low

Sports Ground

P

Recreation Ground

School

MANOR STREET

WILLIAM STREET

ELSING ST

EDWARD ST

MAUD ST

GEORGE ST

DUNCAN ST

LEOPO

MILLICENT ST

KENT ST

CLARENCE ROAD

ADRIAN ST

FREDERICK ST

BEVILLE ST

HELENA ST

STANIER ST

HAYFIELD CRES

MORVILLE CL

ALFRED ST

DEWSBURY ROAD

Fenton Park

Bowling Green

Cemetery

BASSILOW ROAD

ERNEST ST

INKERMAN ST

BROADLANE ST

WARRINGTON STREET

WILEMAN ST

VIVIAN ROAD

STREET

Fenton Low

Fenton

Berry Hill

BREWSTER ROAD
GRAHAM ST
TONE CL
BROUGHTON ROAD
OPHAM PL
ST B5040
TRENTWAY CL
FENTON ROAD
HYNDLEY RD
DAVY CL
CL
WILLETON ST
STAVELEY ST
MALTHOUSE
Sch
FOUNDRY LA
ROAD

DIVIDY ROAD

ELLISON ST

DAVENTRY ST
WEIGHTON CL

KEYWORTH WK
MEWS

BLMHURST CL

CANFORD CL
DORKING ST
DEBENHAM
KETFORD ST
KETTERING

HAMMERTON AV

WALCOT GRO
EAST DEAN
KOLBEACH AV
KILBURN PL
LOW AV
DRAYTON
DEBEYN AV
KETTERING DRIVE

Schools

ASHFIELD SQUARE

TOULON DRI

DEBENHAM CRESCENT

HILLSBERY CL

ARBOURFIELD DRIVE

School

Playing Field

LONGFORD WK

LONGNOR PL
STRAND CL
SOUTH ALL WY
GLENROYD AV
BURFORD WY

Clinic

HOVERINGHAM DRIVE

BRINKHAM CL
SLAPTON CL
RENOWN CL
DRAKE CL
LISKEARD CL
TULSA CL

WILLIAM BIRCH RD

WILLIAM BIRCH CT

ACHILLES WY
AJAX WY

A   B   38   C   D

FENTON PARK
ALFRETON ROAD
ELBURTON ROAD
KELMAN RD
SHARDLOW CL
FENPARK

31

1 2 3 4 5 6

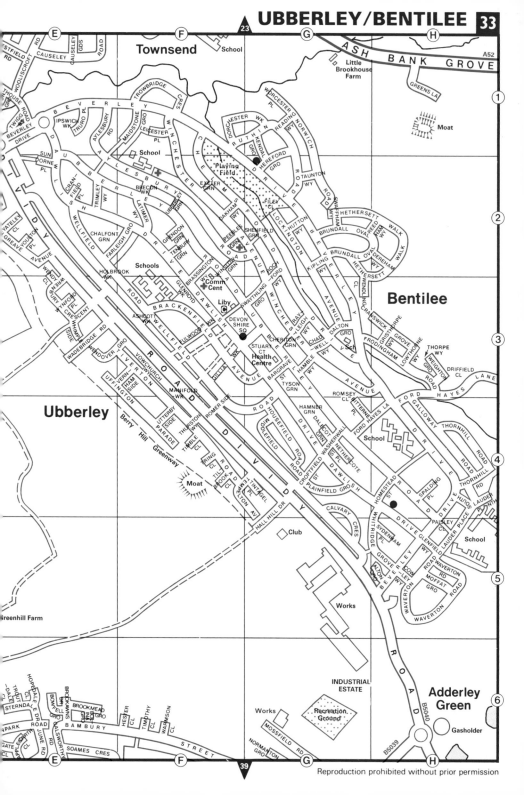

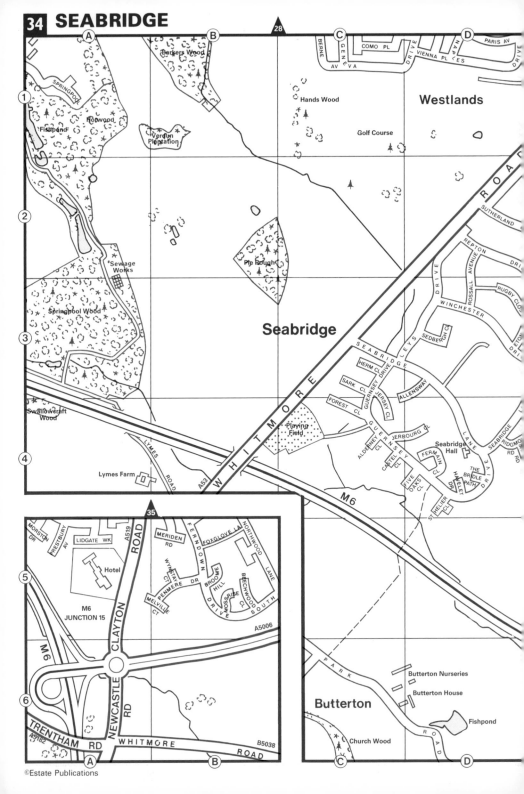

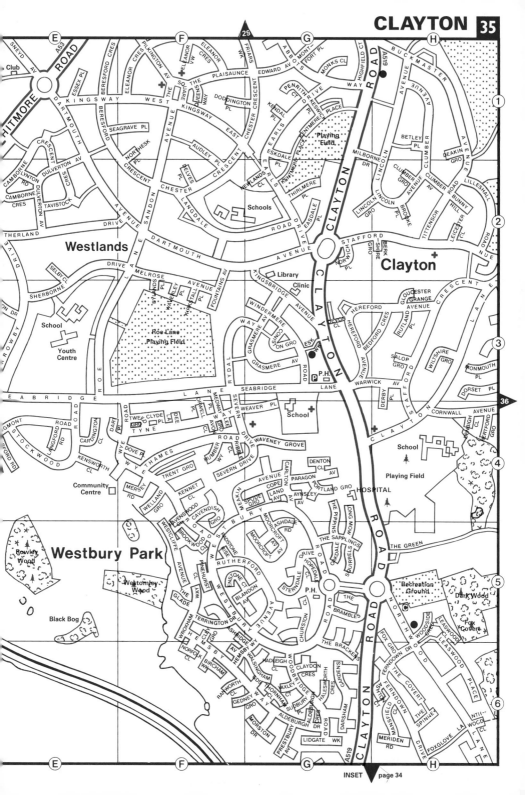

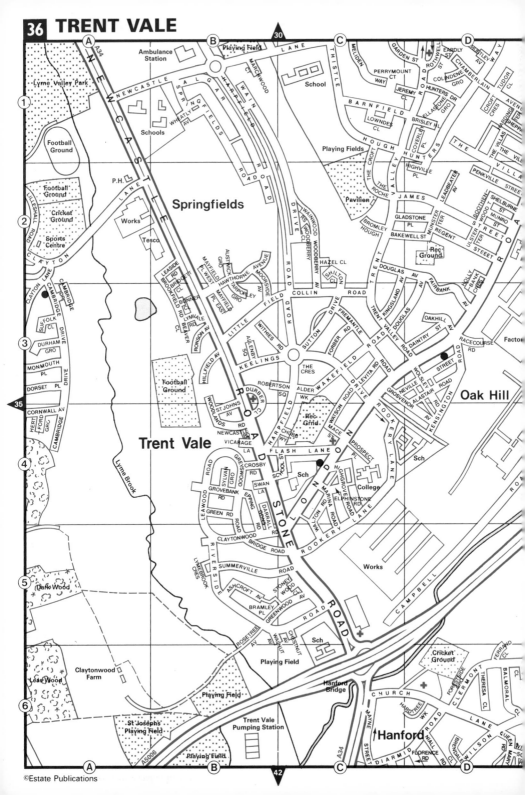

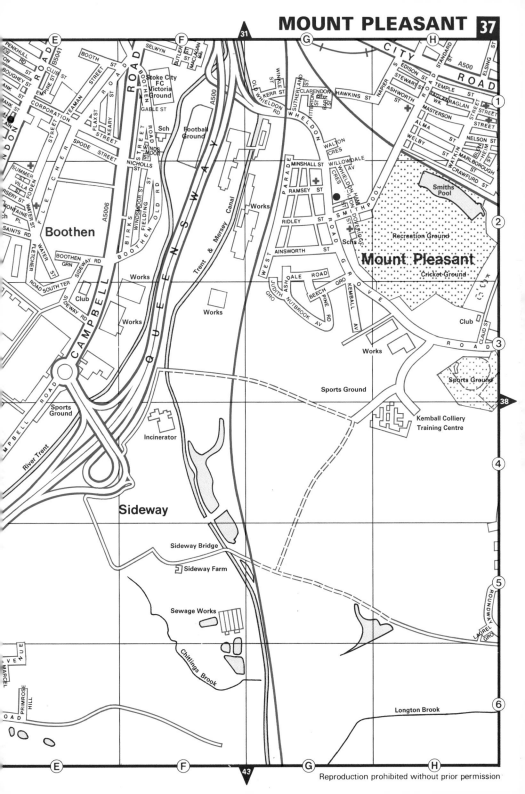

CITY ROAD

A500

E F 31 G H

PENKHULL
BOUGHEY
BANK ST
BANK ST
MAIN
ROAD
B5041
EMPIRE ST
CLUB ST
BOOTH ST
CORPORATION ST
SELWYN ST
BUTLER ST
MACLAGAN ST
Stoke City FC Victoria Ground
OLD WHELDON RD
KERR ST
WINKLE ST
SUTHERLAND RD
CLARENDON
HAWKINS ST
NAPIER ST
ASHWORTH ST
STEWART ST
TEMPLE ST
STANDARD
ELSING ST
EDISON ST
RAGLAN WK
RAGLAN ST
TEMPLE ST
STREET ST
1

SUMMER ST
VILLA
FODEN ST
NURSERY ST
FONTAINE PL
SAINTS RD
FLETCHER
FLAX ST
SPODE STREET
STREET
YEAMAN ST
LEARY ST
STREET
GABLE ST
Sch
NICHOLLS
A5006
FIELDING ST
WINDSMOOR ST
BIRKS ST
ROAD
BOOTHEN OLD RD
Football Ground
A500
WHELDON
ROAD
MASTERSON ST
ALMA ST
WELBY ST
WATKIN ST
HEIM
MARLBOROUGH
CRAWFURD ST
NELSON ST
STREET
2

Boothen

BOOTHEN GRN
SIDEWAY RD
Club
Works
Works
Works
MINSHALL ST
WILLOWDALE AV
WALTON CRES
WILLOWDALE CRES
PARADE
RAMSEY ST
RIDLEY ST
AINSWORTH ST
HAM
SMITH POOL
DOVERIDGE ROAD
HAMIL ST
ROAD
Smiths Pool
Recreation Ground
Mount Pleasant
Cricket Ground
2

CAMPBELL ROAD
Trent & Mersey Canal
QUEENSWAY
WEST
ASHDALE ROAD
JUDITH GRO
NUTBROOK AV
BEECH GRO
PINE RD
KEMBALL AV
GROVE
Schs
Club
CLAUD ST
ROAD
3

Works
Sports Ground
Works
Sports Ground
38

CAMPBELL ROAD
Sports Ground
River Trent
Incinerator
Sports Ground
Kemball Colliery Training Centre
4

Sideway

Sideway Bridge
Sideway Farm
ROUNDWAY
LAUREL GRO
5

Sewage Works
Chitlings Brook
4

VENUE
MARCEL
PRIMROSE HILL
ROAD
Longton Brook
6

E F 43 G H

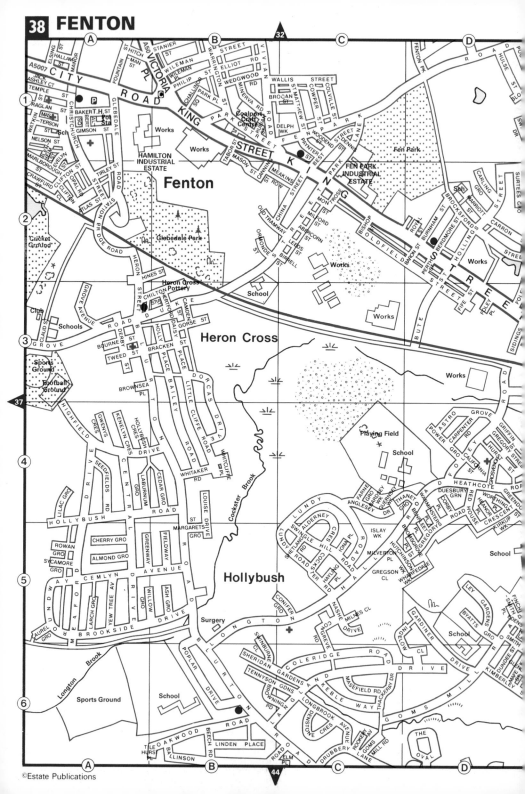

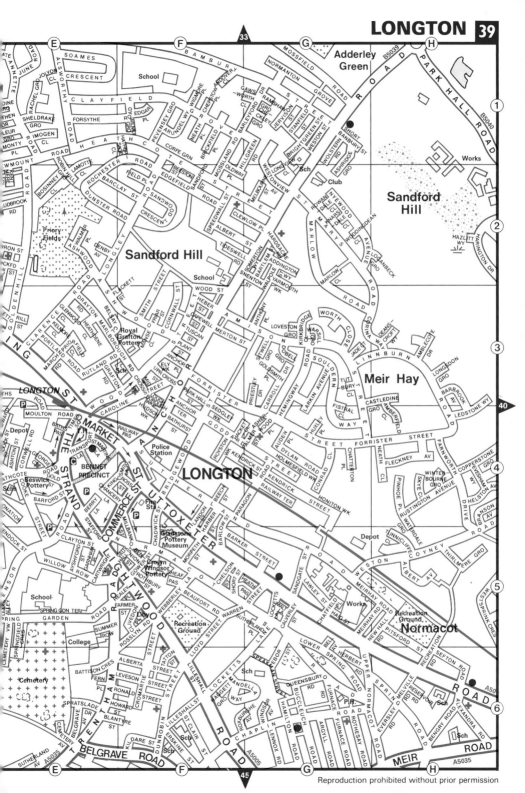

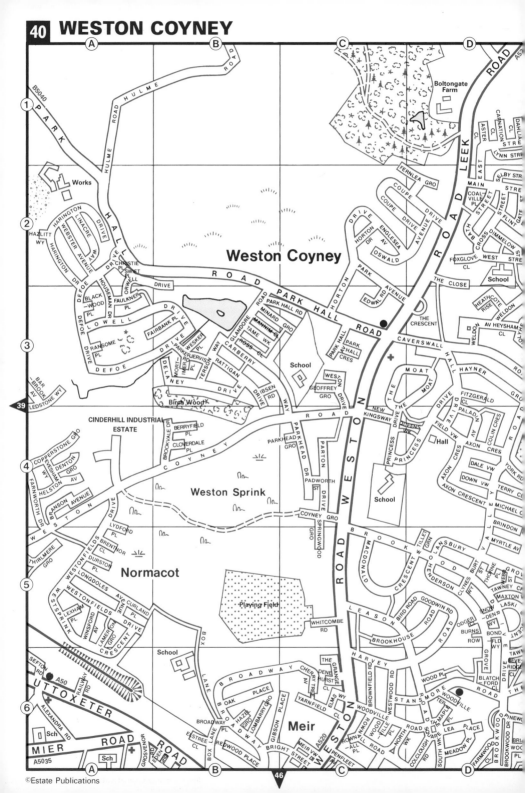

©Estate Publications

Roughcote

Roughcote Hall Farm

Caverswall Common

Mount Pleasant Farm

Hardiwick

Intakes Farm

Green Farm

Cookshill

Cookshill Hall

Vicarage Farm

Finger Post Farm

Swan Bank (motte)

School

Caverswall

School

Grave Yard

Caverswall Cricket Ground

River Blythe

Convent

Castle

Dove House Farm

Playing Field

School

Police Office

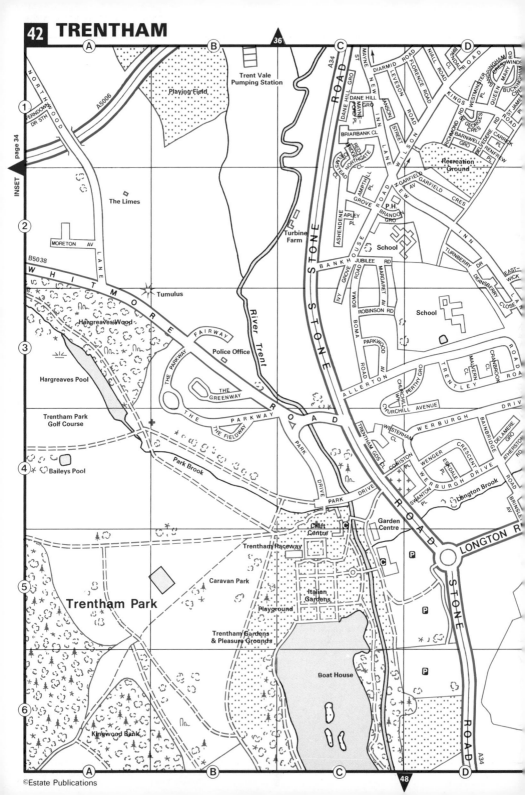

Trentham

Trentham

Hem Heath

Trentham Ley

Trentham Golf Course

Playing Field

School

Depot

British Coal

Cricket Ground

Football Ground

NEWSTEAD

PLANTATION ROAD

TRADING ESTATE

ALDERFLAT DRIVE

Club House

Rugby Ground

New Park

Blurton

Newstead

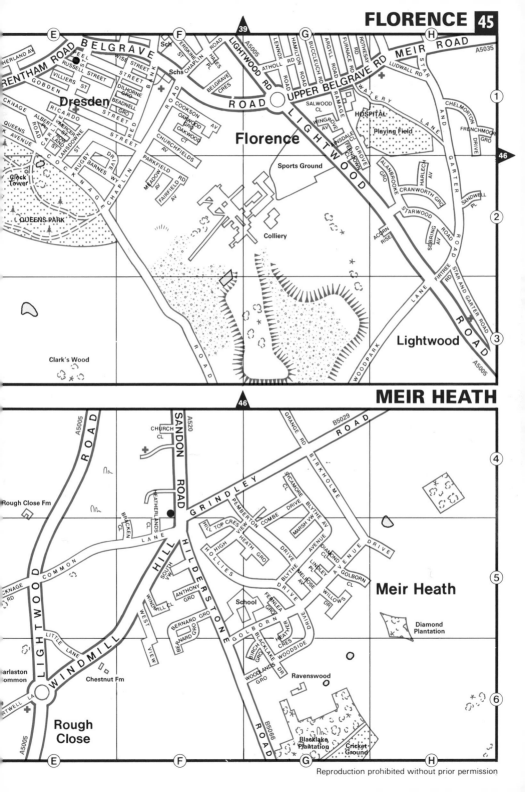

MEIR HEATH

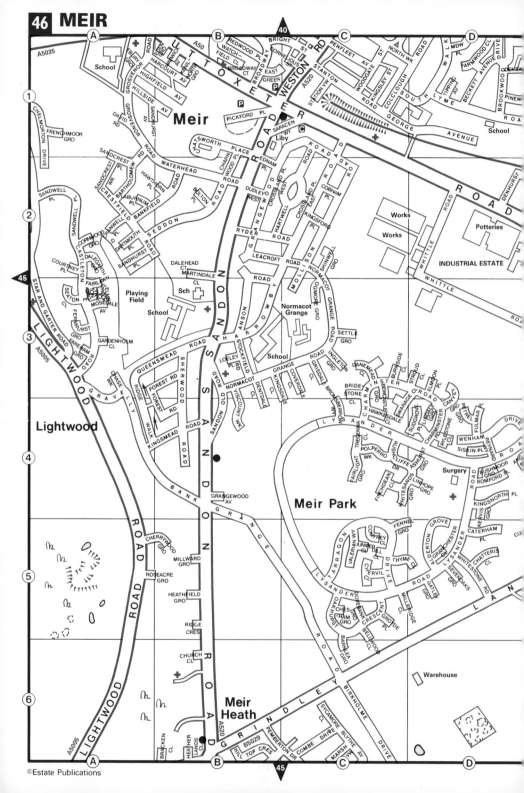

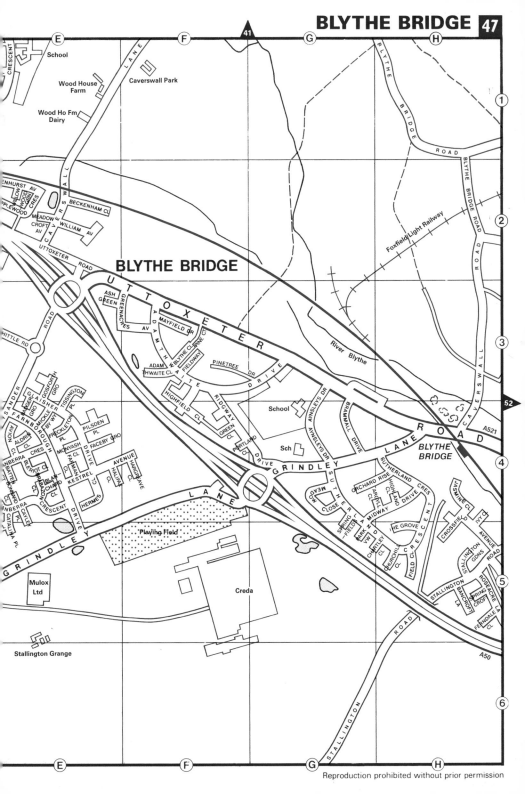

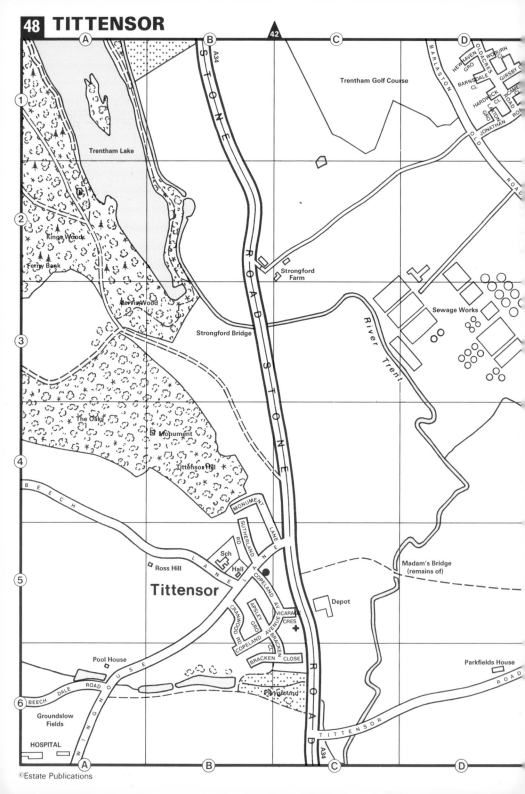

48 TITTENSOR

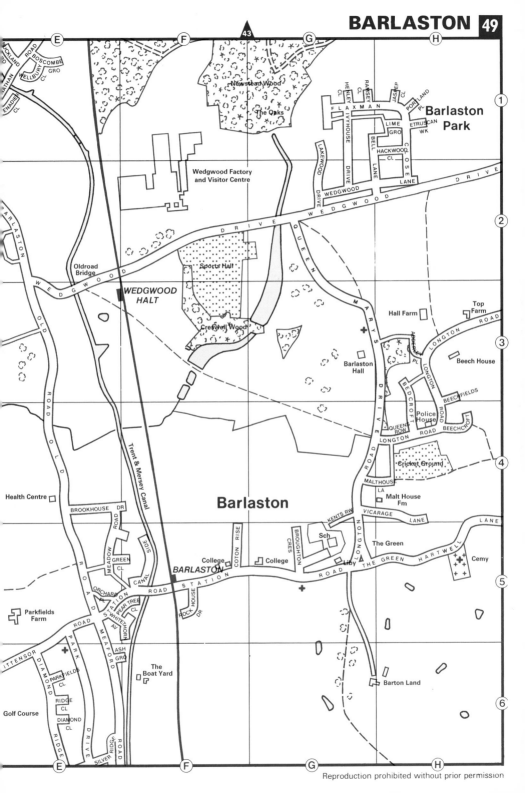

BARLASTON
49

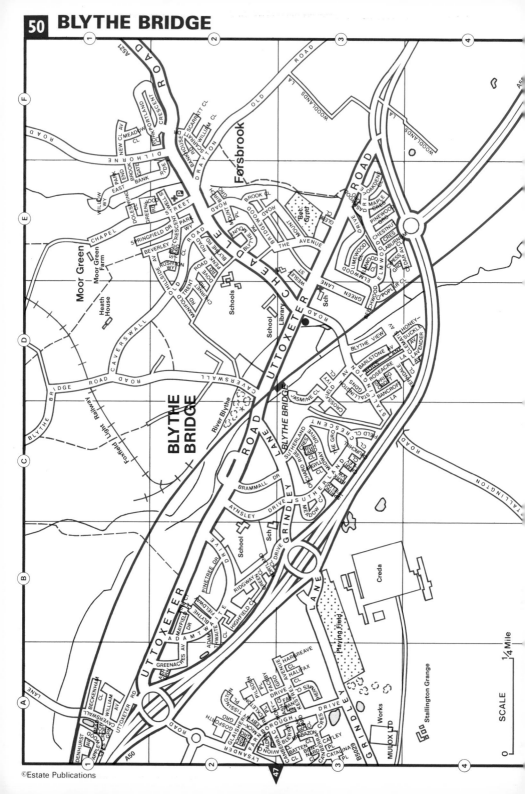

Forsbrook

Moor Green

Moor Green Farm

Heath House

BLYTHE BRIDGE

River Blythe

Foxfield Light Railway

Schools

School

Library

Sch

Creda

Playing Field

Stallington Grange

Works

MULOX LTD

School

Sch

SCALE

0   1/4 Mile

47

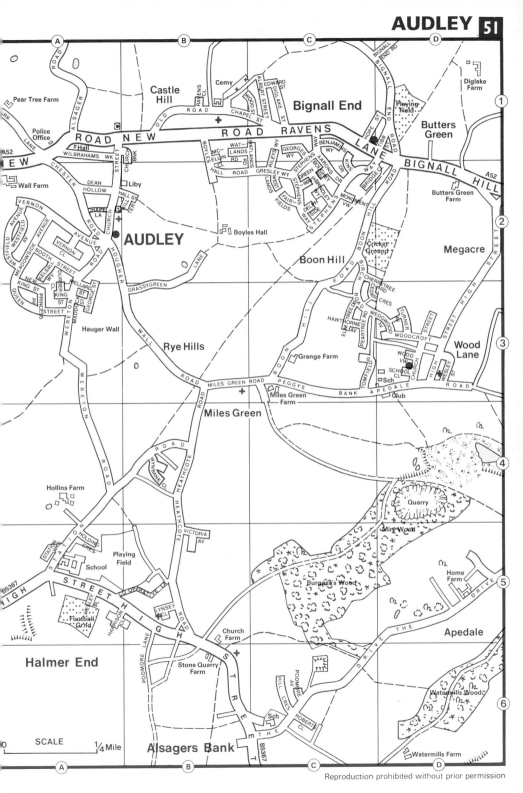

Pear Tree Farm

Police Office

Wall Farm

A52

NEW

CHESTER

ROAD NEW

WILBRAHAMS WK

Hall

DEAN HOLLOW

HALL RD

Liby

CHAPEL LA

ALSAGER

ROAD

OLD ROAD

CHURCH STREET

HILL TERR

HOUGHER LANE

VERNON AVENUE

WESTFIELD

MEADOWSIDE AV

VERNON CL

BOOTH AVENUE

KELSALL

DURBER CL

GEORGES ST

MADDOCKS

KING ST

NEW KING ST

QUEEN AV

PRINCES ST

WERETON

WALL ROAD

AUDLEY

Castle Hill

Cemy

RAVENS CL

WOOD ST

CHAPEL ST

ALBERT STREET

EDWARD ST

DIGLAKE ST

ROAD RAVENS

BOYLES HALL

MC-LELLIN CL

WAT-LANDS RD

WATLANDS RD

RILEY ST

GEORGE WY

STEPHENS WY

GRESLEY WY

WEST STEPHENS

FAIR-FIELDS

STEPHENS WAY

DELPH SIDE

AARONS DR

BENJAMINS WY

BRADLEY WY

STEPHEN ST

BOYLES

BRIDGE ST

KINS WY

MONUMENT VW

BIGNALL END RD

BIGNALL END RD

HOPE ST

TIBB ST

LANE

Bignall End

Playing Field

Butters Green

Butters Green Farm

BIGNALL HILL

A52

HIGH STREET

Megacre

Boyles Hall

AUDLEY

Hauger Wall

GRASSYGREEN LANE

Rye Hills

WERETON ROAD

WALL ROAD

MILES GREEN ROAD

0

Miles Green

Boon Hill

BOON HILL ROAD

Grange Farm

ELM DR

HAWTHORNE AV

FREDA DR

PEARTREE RD

CHERRY TREE

CROFT

CRES

WEDGWOOD

HIGH

TURNER

WOODCROFT

TOMFIELDS

Sch

SCHOOL CL

WOOD VW

CHURCH STREET

WESLEY ST

HIGH STREET

Wood Lane

PEGGYS BANK

APEDALE ROAD

Miles Green Farm

Club

Hollins Farm

HEATHCOTE

ROAD

WYNBANK CL

HEATHCOTE

VICTORIA AV

HOLDING CRES

STATION WK

Playing Field

School

B5367

HIGH

STREET HILL

WESLEY ST

Halmer End

Football Grnd

HARRISON

PODMORE LANE

CO-OPERATIVE LA

LYNSEY CL

HIGH STREET

Church Farm

Stone Quarry Farm

Sch

HILL CRES

PODMORE AV

ROBERTS CL

THE

B5367

Alsagers Bank

Quarry

Miry Wood

Burgess's Wood

THE DRIVE

Home Farm

DRIVE

Apedale

Watermills Wood

Watermills Farm

Diglake Farm

INDEX TO STREETS

Maureen Av 7 G5
Meadows Rd 6 D2
Medina Way 7 E2
Merelake Rd 6 A4
Mill Rise 6 D3
Millers View 6 D3
Millstone Av 6 B2
Milton Cres 6 A4
Minfield Clo 7 E4
Mistley Walk 7 F4
Mitchell Av 6 B3
Mitchell Dri 6 B3
Mobberley Rd 7 F4
Monument Rd 6 B6
Moreton Clo 7 E4
Moss Pl 7 E1
Mount Pleasant 7 E3
Mount Rd 7 E2
Murray St 7 G5
Nabbswood Rd 7 F2
Napier Gdns 7 E2
Nelson Bank 6 D4
Newark Gro 7 G5
Newcastle Rd 6 B4
Newchapel Rd 7 F1
Norfolk Rd 6 D2
Old Butt La 6 A2
Oldcott Cres 7 F4
Oldcott Dri 7 F4
Oldhill Clo 6 B6
Orchard Cres 6 B3
Park Av 6 C4
Park Farm View 7 G5
Park View Rd 7 E1
Parklands 7 E2
Peakdale Av 7 F5
Peckforton View 7 E4
Pennyfields Rd 7 G2
Perkins St 7 F5
Pickwick Pl 6 B2
Pine Clo 6 A5
Pit La 6 A6
Poplar Dri 7 E3
Powy Dri 7 E2
Princess St 6 B6
Priory Pl 7 F1
Quarry Ter 7 E3
Queen St 6 D2
Queens Gdns 6 B6
Randel La 7 F4
Ravenscliffe Rd 6 D4
Rectory View 6 B5
Red Lion Clo 6 B4
Regency Clo 6 B6
Ridge Rd 7 G6
Rigby Rd 7 F1
Rockhouse La 6 A4
Rodgers St 7 F4
Rookery Rd 7 F1
Rowan Clo 7 E4
Russell Pl 7 H6
Russell Rd 7 H6
Rutland Rd 7 E1
St Andrews Dri 7 F1
St Johns Wood 6 D3
St Martins Rd 6 B6
St Saviours St 6 B3
Salop Pl 7 E1
Sandy Rd 7 G5
Second Av 6 C3
Shakespeare Clo 6 D3
Shannon Dri 7 F4
Shelford Rd 7 G6
Shelley Clo 6 D4
Silverwood 7 F2
Skellern St 6 B2
Slacken La 6 B2
Sneyd Pl 7 G6
Somerset Av 6 D2
Spey Dri 7 F1
Spout Hollow 6 B6
Springhead Clo 6 B6
Station Rd, Kidsgrove 6 D2
Station Rd, Newchapel 7 H2
Stone Bank Rd 7 E3
Summerfield 7 E3
Surrey Rd 7 E2
Sussex Dri 6 D1
Swallow Clo 7 E2
Swallowmore View 6 A4
Swan Bank 6 A5
Swan Clo 6 B4
Swift Clo 7 E2
Sycamore Clo 6 C4
Tamar Rd 7 E2
Target Clo 6 B6
Tawney Clo 7 F1
Taylor St 7 G5
Telford Clo 6 C3
Temperance Pl 7 G5
Tennyson Av 6 D4
Tern Av 7 G2
The Avenue 6 D3
The Mount 7 E3
Third Av 6 C2
Thomas St 6 B4
Tilewright Clo 7 E2
Tilstone Clo 7 E3
Tollgate Clo 6 A4
Townfield Clo 6 B2
Trubshaw Pl 7 F1
Unity Way 6 B4
Valentine Rd 7 E3
Victoria Av 6 D2
Vine Bank Rd 7 E2
Walley Dri 7 G6
Walton Gro 6 A4
Walton Way 6 A4
Warwick Clo 6 D1
Wedgwood Rd 6 B5
Weetman Clo 7 F4
Weir Gro 7 E2
Wellington Rd 7 E2
Wentworth Dri 7 G1
Wesley Gdns 7 E2
West Av 6 A3
Westmorland Av 6 C4
Wheelock Way 7 E2
Whitehall Av 6 D2
Whitehall Rd 6 D2
Whitehill Rd 7 E2
Whiteridge Rd 7 E2
Wignall Rd 7 G5
William Rd 7 E1
Willow Clo 6 D4
Wilson Way 7 F5
Windmill Av 7 E3
Woodhall Gdns 7 F1
Woodlands Av 6 B2
Woodshutts St 6 B2
Woodside Av 6 D3
Woodstock Rd 7 E5
Woodstock St 7 F4
Worcester Clo 6 B5
Wright St 6 B2
Yew Tree Ter 6 D4
York Clo 6 B4

STOKE-ON-TRENT

Abbey La 22 D4
Abbey Rd 22 D3
Abbey St, Abbey Hulton 22 D3
Abbey St, Silverdale 27 H3
Abbots Pl 22 D2
Abbots Rd 22 D2
Abbots Way 29 F6
Abbotts Dri 16 A6
Abercorn St 38 C2
Aberford Gro 22 B3
Abingdon Way 43 F4
Acacia Av 28 C1
Acacia Gro 28 C1
Achilles Way 32 C2
Acorn Rise 45 H2
Acreswood Rd 15 E3
Acton St 21 H3
Adams Av 8 A6
Adams St, May Bank 19 H5
Adams St, Milton 17 E5
Adamthwaite Clo 47 F3
Adamthwaite Dri 47 F3
Adderley Pl 49 H3
Adderley Rd 16 A2
Addington Way 39 G2
Addison St 21 H3
Adelaide St 14 D6
Adkins St 21 F1
Adrian St 32 A6
Adventure Pl 21 G6
Aegean Gro 43 F2
Ageling Grn 16 B6
Agger Hill 26 A3
Ainsbury Gro 41 E5
Ainsdale Clo 45 G1
Ainsworth St 37 G2
Aintree Clo 43 E3
Aitken St 14 B6
Ajax Way 32 C2
Alan Dale 24 D4
Alanbrooke Gro 45 H2
Alanley Clo 15 H5
Alastair Rd 36 D3
Albany Gro 30 A4
Albany Rd, Hartshill 30 B4
Albany Rd, Newcastle 29 F2
Albemarle Rd 19 E6
Albert Av 39 H5
Albert Pl 45 E1
Albert Rd 43 F5
Albert Sq 38 A1
Albert St, Beasley 18 C2
Albert St, Newcastle 30 A3
Albert St, Sandford Hill 39 F2
Albert St, Silverdale 28 A2
Albert Ter 19 G3
Alberta St 39 F6
Albion Sq 21 G6
Albion St 21 G6
Alcester Clo 9 F4
Aldbury Pl 44 A2
Aldeburgh Cres 35 G6
Aldeburgh Dri 35 G6
Alder Gro 12 B6
Alder Walk 36 C3
Alderflat Dri 43 H4
Alderney Clo 34 C4
Alderney Cres 38 C5
Alderton Gro 46 D5
Aldrin Clo 47 E4
Alexandra Rd, Dimsdale 19 H4
Alexandra Rd, Normacot 39 H6
Alford Dri 24 C5
Alfred St 32 A5
Alfreton Rd 32 D6
Algar Rd 36 B1
All Saints Rd 37 E2
Allen St 30 C4
Allenby Sq 36 B3
Allendale Walk 44 B1
Allensmore Av 39 E2
Allensway 34 D3
Allerton Rd 42 C3
Alma St 37 H1
Almer Pl 8 D5
Almond Gro 38 A5
Almond Pl 12 C4
Alstonfield Av 23 F2
Alton Clo 27 G3
Alton Gro 33 H5
Alwyn Cres 15 H6
Amberfield Clo 39 H4
Amblecote Dri 39 H3
Ambleside Pl 14 D2
Ambrose Pl 8 C3
America St 14 A1
Amicable St 20 C1
Amison St 39 F3
Ampthill Pl 42 C2
Anchor Pl 39 F3
Anchor Rd 39 F4
Anchor Ter 39 F4
Anderson Pl 16 B2
Andover Clo 39 F1
Andrew Pl 29 H3
Anglesey Dri 38 C4
Angus Clo 23 F6
Anna Walk 20 D1
Annette Rd 39 E1
Ansmede Gro 44 C1
Anson Rd 46 B3
Anthony Gro 45 F5
Anthony Pl 39 G3
Anthonys Dri 29 E6
Apedale Rd 18 B2
Apley Pl 42 C2
Apollo Walk 15 G5
Applecroft 12 C5
Appledore Gro 8 C2
Appleford Pl 44 A1
Applegarth Clo 33 E6
Applewood Cres 47 E2
Apsley Gro 48 B5
Aquinas St 31 E5
Arbour St 21 G4
Arbourfield Dri 32 D2
Arclid Way 32 D2
Arctic Pl 43 F3
Argosy Clo 46 D4
Argyle St 31 E1
Argyll Clo 47 H4
Argyll Rd 39 G6
Aries Clo 8 C4
Arkwright Gro 16 B6
Armshead Rd 24 C2
Armstrong Grn 21 G1
Arnold Gro 19 F1
Arran Dri 8 C2
Arthur St, Newcastle 28 D2
Arthur St, Tunstall 14 B1
Arundel Way 39 F1
Ash Bank Rd 24 A5
Ash Green 47 E3
Ash Gro, Ash Bank 24 B5
Ash Gro, Barlaston 49 E6
Ash Gro, Hollybush 38 B5
Ash Gro, Silverdale 27 G2
Ash Way 24 B6
Ashbourne Dri 27 G3
Ashbourne Gro 21 F3
Ashburton St 21 E1
Ashby Cres 44 B1
Ashcombe Grn 44 C1
Ashcott Walk 33 F3
Ashcroft Av 36 B5
Ashcroft Clo 19 F3
Ashcroft Gro 19 F2
Ashcroft Oval 19 F2
Ashcroft Pl 19 F2
Ashcroft Rd 19 F3
Ashdale Rd, Mount Pleasant 37 G3
Ashdale Rd, Westbury Park 35 G5
Ashendene Gro 42 C2
Asherwood Pl 39 G4
Ashfield Square 32 D1
Ashfields New Rd 29 F2
Ashford St 31 F3
Ashgreen Clo 43 E4
Ashlands Av 30 B4
Ashlands Cres 30 B4
Ashlands Gro 30 B5
Ashlands Rd 30 B4
Ashlar Clo 8 D2
Ashley Gro 19 H5
Ashley St 31 F1
Ashman St 15 G3
Ashridge Av 35 F5
Ashridge Gro 39 G1
Ashton Ct, Washerwall 24 C5
Ashton Ct, Westbury Park 35 H6
Ashton St 39 E4
Ashurst Gro 46 D4
Ashwell Rd 30 A4
Ashwood 39 E2
Ashwood Gro 50 E3
Ashworth St 37 H1
Aster Clo 40 D1
Astro Gro 38 D4
Athelstan St 14 A1
Athena Rd 22 B3
Atherston Rd 42 D4
Athlone St 15 H4
Atholl Rd 45 G1
Atlam Clo 22 C6
Atlantic Gro 43 F2
Atlas St 38 A2
Auckland St 14 D6
Auden Pl 39 G4
Audley Pl 35 F1
Audley Rd 12 A4
Audley St, Knutton 28 C1
Audley St, Tunstall 14 A2
Austin St 32 A2
Austwick Gro 36 B2
Aveling Rd 16 B6
Avenue Rd 31 F3
Avion Clo 47 E4
Avoca St 21 H3
Avon Clo 35 F4
Avondale St 14 A6
Avonside Av 8 D6
Axon Cres 40 D4
Aylesbury Rd 33 E1
Aynesley Rd 31 E3
Aynsley Av 35 G4
Aynsleys Dri 47 G4
Ayshford St 39 E5
Back Bunts La 17 G1
Back Ford Grn Rd 15 G3
Back La 11 E1
Back La, Brown Edge 11 E3
Baddeley Green La 17 E4
Baddeley Hall Rd 17 F3
Baddeley Rd 17 E4
Baddeley St 14 D5
Baden Rd 15 G4
Baden St 29 F2
Badger Gro 47 E4
Baggott Pl 28 D4
Bagnall Rd 17 E5
Bagnall St 21 G6
Bagot Gro 16 B6
Bailey Rd 38 B3
Bailey St, Newcastle 29 F3
Bailey St, Cliff Vale 30 C2
Bainbridge Rd 42 D4
Bainsgrove 13 E6
Baker Cres 17 E2
Baker Cres Nth 17 E2
Baker Cres Sth 17 E3
Baker St 38 A1
Bakewell Clo 27 G3
Balfour St 21 H6
Ball Green Rd 10 A5
Ball Hayes Rd 9 F6
Ball La 10 C6
Ballinson Rd 38 B6
Balliol St 30 D5
Balloon St 30 A3
Balls Yard 29 G3
Balmoral Clo 36 D6
Baltic Clo 43 F3
Bamber Pl 19 E2
Bamber St 31 E5
Bambury Rd 39 F1
Bamford Gro 21 F4
Bancroft La 50 D3
Bank Hall Rd 15 F3
Bank House Dri 30 B2
Bank St 14 A1
Bankfield Rd 46 A2
Bankhouse Rd, Forsbrook 50 F2
Bankhouse Rd, Trentham 42 C2
Bankside 29 H4
Banktop Av 15 E2
Baptist St 14 D6
Barber Pl 8 D4
Barber Rd 8 D4
Barber St 14 C4
Barbridge Rd 12 B4
Barbrook Av 39 H3
Barclay St 39 E2
Bardsey Walk 38 C4
Barford Dri 35 E4
Barford St 39 E4
Bargrave St 33 G3
Barker St, Broad Meadow 18 D3
Barker St, Longton 39 F5
Barkers Sq 20 A4
Barks Dri 9 H6
Barlaston Old Rd 43 E5
Barlaston Rd 44 C2
Barleyford Dri 39 G1
Barlow St 39 F5
Barlstone Av 50 D3
Barn St 37 G1
Barncroft Rd 9 F5
Barnes Way 45 E2
Barnett Gro 8 C6
Barnfield 36 C2
Barnfield Rd 20 D1
Barnlea Gro 46 C6
Barnsdale Clo 48 D1
Barnwell Gro 42 D1
Barracks Rd 29 G4
Barratt Gdns 17 E5
Barrett Cres 21 E3
Barrett Dri 20 D2
Barrington Ct 20 B6
Barry Av 22 C6
Bartholomew Rd 46 A2
Barthomley Rd 21 H2
Bartlem St 39 G2
Barton Cres 14 B4
Basford Park Rd 30 A1
Baskerville Rd 21 H4
Baskeyfield Pl 9 F5
Basnetts Wood Rd 11 H4
Bassilow Rd 32 B6
Bath Rd 27 E1
Bath St, Stoke 31 E6
Bath St, West Coyney 40 D2
Bath Ter 31 E6
Baths Pas 39 E4
Baths Rd 39 E3
Bathurst St 39 F4
Batten Ct 47 E4
Battison Cres 39 E6
Bay Tree Clo 22 B3
Bayham Walk 22 D5
Beaconsfield 19 G2
Beaconsfield Dri 44 A2
Beadnell Gro 45 F1
Beard Gro 22 D1
Beasley Av 18 D2
Beasley Pl 18 D1
Beattie Av 29 G1
Beauford Av 24 C5
Beaufort Rd 39 F5
Beaulieu Clo 24 D6
Beaumaris Clo 30 A4
Beaumaris Ct 29 E5
Beaumont Rd 14 B2
Beaver Clo 36 B3
Beckenham Clo 47 E2
Beckett Av 46 D1
Beckford St 21 H4
Beckton Av 14 C2
Bedale Pl 44 A1
Bedcroft 49 H4
Bedford Cres 35 G3
Bedford Rd 31 E2
Bedford St 31 E2
Beech Dale Rd 48 A6
Beech Gro 37 G3
Beech La 48 A4
Beech Rd 38 B6
Beech St 39 F4
Beechcroft 49 H4
Beeches Row 8 A5
Beechfield Rd 43 F5
Beechfields 49 H3
Beechmont Gro 22 B3
Beechwood Clo, Blythe Bridge 50 D3

Beechwood Clo, Westbury Park 34 B5
Beeston St 39 F2
Belfast Clo 15 F3
Belfield Av 19 H5
Belford Pl 30 C3
Belgrave Av 39 E6
Belgrave Cres 45 F1
Belgrave Rd, Florence 39 E6
Belgrave Rd, Newcastle 29 H4
Bell Av 39 G5
Bell La 49 G1
Bellerton La 16 A3
Bells Hollow 12 B3
Bellwood Clo 46 C5
Belmont Rd 30 D1
Belsay Clo 39 E3
Belvedere Rd 42 D1
Belvoir Av 43 F6
Bemersley Rd 9 H1
Benectine Pl 22 D4
Benfleet Pl 38 D5
Bengal Gro 43 F2
Bengry Rd 39 H6
Bennet Precinct 39 E4
Bennett Pl 19 G1
Bennett St 20 C1
Bennion St 39 F5
Benson St 8 C5
Bentley Av 19 F5
Bentley Rd 9 G5
Berdmore St 38 D2
Beresford Cres 35 E1
Beresford St 31 F3
Berkeley St 31 H1
Bernard Gro 45 F5
Bernard St 31 H1
Berne Av 28 C6
Berry La 39 E4
Berry St 31 E5
Berryfield Pl 40 B4
Berwick Rd 16 A5
Berwick Walks 28 D5
Best St 38 C1
Beswick Rd 8 D5
Bethesda Rd 31 G2
Bethesda St 21 G6
Betley Pl 35 H1
Bettany Rd 21 E1
Bevandean Clo 43 G6
Beveridge Clo 40 D6
Beverley Cres 50 E2
Beverley Dri 33 E1
Beville St 32 B6
Bevin La 22 D6
Bew Hall Rd 39 H5
Bew St 10 A5
Bewcastle Gro 46 C3
Bexhill Gro 22 C3
Bexley St 21 F4
Biddulph Rd 8 D4
Billinge St 14 C6
Bilton St 37 E1
Birch Green Gro 22 A2
Birch Gro, Forsbrook 50 E2
Birch Gro, Meir Heath 45 G6
Birch House Rd 12 B6
Birch St 22 A4
Birch Ter 21 G6
Birch Walk 44 C1
Bircham Walk 35 F6
Birchdown Av 15 E2
Birchenwood Rd 8 B2
Birches Head Rd 21 H3
Birchfield Rd 23 F3
Birchgate 23 F5
Birchgate Gro 23 F5
Birchlands Rd 22 B3
Birchover Walk 9 E2
Bird Cage Walk 21 F6
Bird Rd 40 C5
Birkett St 21 F5
Birkholme Dri 45 G4
Birks St 37 F2
Birrell St 38 C2
Biscay Gro 43 F2
Bishop Rd 9 E5
Bishop St 38 C2
Bitterne Pl 33 G4
Blackbank Rd 28 A1
Blackfriars Rd 29 F4
Blackhorse La 21 F5
Blacklake Dri 45 G5
Blackthorn Pl 12 C5
Blackwells Row 21 F3
Blackwood Pl 40 A3
Bladon Clo 9 E2
Blake St 14 C6
Blakelow Rd 22 D3
Blanchard Clo 47 E4
Blandon Av 35 G5
Blantyre St 39 E6
Blatchford Clo 40 D6
Bleak Pl 21 E1
Bleak St 20 A6
Blencarn Gro 17 F1
Blenheim St 37 H2
Bleriot Clo 47 E4
Blithfield Clo 24 C6
Bluestone Av 15 F4
Blunt St 19 H5
Blurton Rd, Heron Cross 38 A3
Blurton Rd, Newstead 44 C5
Blythe Av 45 G4
Blythe Bridge Rd 50 C1
Blythe Clo 47 F3
Blythe Mount Pk 50 E2
Blythe Rd 50 E2
Blythe View 50 D3
Bogs La 50 D3
Bold St 22 A4
Bolina Gro 33 E6
Bolney Gro 22 C3
Bolsover Clo 8 D2
Bolton Pl 46 B2
Boma Rd 42 C3
Bond St 8 A6
Bondfield Way 40 D5
Bonnard Clo 47 E4
Bonner Clo 36 B3
Boon Av 30 D6
Booth St, Broad Meadow 18 D3
Booth St, Stoke 37 E1
Boothen Grn 37 E2
Boothen Old Rd 37 F2
Boothen Rd 37 F1
Boothenwood Ter 36 D2
*Boothroyd St, Bagnall St 21 G6
Borough Rd 29 H3
Borrowdale Rd 16 A2
Boscombe Gro 49 E1
Bosinney Clo 39 E2
Boswell St 30 C2
Botany Bay Rd 22 A4
Botteslow St 21 H6
Boughey Rd 31 G4
Boughey St 37 E1
Boulton St, Birches Head 21 H3
Boulton St, Dimsdale 19 H3
Boundary St, Hanley 21 F4
Boundary St, Hartshill 30 A3
Bourne St 38 A3
Bournes Bank 14 D6
Bouverie Par 16 B6
Bow St 21 G4
Bow Wood Pl 12 B5
Bowden St 15 E4
Bower St 31 G2
Bowfell Gro 33 E6
Bowland Av 28 C1
Bowman Gro 9 F2
Bowmead Clo 43 G4
Bowns St 21 F3
Bowstead St 31 F6
Bowyer Av 10 A5
Box La 40 B5
Brabazone Clo 47 E4
Bracken Clo, Meir Heath 45 F5
Bracken Clo, Tittensor 48 B6
Bracken St 38 B3
Brackenberry 29 G1
Brackenfield Av 33 F3
Brackley Av 15 F4
Bradbury Clo 16 B2
Bradford Ter 22 A3
Bradwell Grange 19 G2
Bradwell La 19 E1
Bradwell Lodge 19 G2
Bradwell St 14 A6
Braemar Clo 23 G6
Braemore Rd 23 E2
Braitwell Dri 16 D3
Bramfield Dri 29 G2
Bramley Pl 36 B5
Brammall Dri 47 G4
Brammer St 15 F2
Brampton Gdns 29 H1
Brampton Rd 29 H2
Brampton Sidings 29 G2
Brandon Gro 42 C2
Branson Av 39 H4
Bransty Gro 43 G6
Brant Av 19 F5
Brassington Way 33 F2
Bream Way 15 F3
Brecon Walk 33 F2
Breedon Clo 18 D6
Breeze Av 8 B6
Brendale Clo 36 D6
Brentnor Clo 40 A5
Brentwood Dri 24 D4
Brentwood Gro 17 F2
Brereton Pl 14 B5
Bretherton Pl 8 D4
Brewery St 21 G4
Brewster Rd 32 C1
Brianson Av 21 G1
Briarbank Clo 42 C1
Briarswood Pl 40 D6
Brick Kiln La 18 C1
Brickfield Pl 39 F1
Brickhouse St 14 D6
Brickkiln La 30 B2
Bridal Pth 24 B5
Bridestone Clo 46 C3
Bridge Rd 35 B5
Bridge St, Newcastle 29 F3
Bridge St, Silverdale 28 A2
Bridgecroft 9 F4
Bridgett Clo 36 B2
Bridgewater St 14 A6
Bridgewood Rd 50 E2
Bridgewood St 39 F4
Bridgnorth Gro 12 C3
Brierley St 15 G4
Brieryhurst Clo 23 F3
Bright St 46 C1
Brightgreen St 39 G1
Brighton St 30 D5
Brindley La 17 F3
Brindley Pl 9 F4
Brindley St 29 F3
Brindon Clo 40 D4
Brindwell Gro 43 G4
Brinsley Av 42 D4
Brisley Hill 36 D1
Bristol St 20 A4
Brittain Av 18 D1
Brittle La 15 H3
Britton St 30 C3
Brixham Clo 32 C3
Broad La 11 E1
Broad St, Newcastle 29 F3
Broad St, Stoke 31 F1
Broadhurst St 15 E4
Broadmans Bank 10 D1
Broadmine St 32 B6
Broadway 40 B6
Broadway Ct 46 B1
Broadway Pl 40 B6
Broakoak Way 44 A2
Brockbank Pl 9 E5
Brocklehurst Way 22 A1
Brockley Sq 21 G5
Brocksford St 38 D2
Brockton Walk 44 A1
Brogan St 38 B1
Bromley Ct 21 E4
Bromley Hough 36 C2
Bromley St 21 E4
Brompton Dri 17 E3
Bromsberrow Way 46 C4
Bromsgrove Pl 38 D5
Brook Clo 50 E2
Brook Gate 50 E1
Brook La 29 G5
Brook Pl 30 C2
Brook Rd 43 E4
Brook St, Silverdale 27 H2
Brook St, Stoke 31 F5
Brooke Pl 35 H2
Brookfield Av 11 H4
Brookfield Rd, Baddeley Edge 17 F2
Brookfield Rd, Trent Vale 36 B3
Brookhouse Dri 49 E4
Brookhouse La 23 G6
Brookhouse Rd, Crackley 12 D5
Brookhouse Rd, Weston Coyney 40 C5
Brookland Rd 8 C5
Brooklands Av 44 D1
Brooklawns Dri 33 E6
Brookmead Gro 33 E6
Brookside Clo 29 E5
Brookside Dri 38 A5
Brookvale Dri 40 B4
Brookwood Clo 35 F5
Brookwood Dri 40 C5
Broom St 21 G4
Broome Hill 34 B5
Broomfield Place Nth 21 E6
Broomfield Place Sth 21 E6
Broomfield Rd 10 A5
Broomhill St 13 H1
Brough La 43 F4
Broughton Cres 49 G5
Broughton Rd, Basford 30 A2
Broughton Rd, Bucknall 32 C1
Brown St 15 E6
Brownfield Rd 40 C6
Brownhill Rd 10 D2
Brownhills Rd 14 B3
Browning Rd 38 B6
Brownley Rd 15 H5
Brownsea Pl 38 A3
Brundall Oval 33 G2
Brunswick Pl 31 G1
Brunswick St, Hanley 21 G5
Brunswick St, Newcastle 29 G3
Brunt St 20 A1
Brutus Rd 18 B3
Bryan St 21 G4
Bryant Pl 23 E5
Bryant Rd 23 E4
Brymbo Rd 18 D4
Buccleuch Rd 39 G6
Buckingham Cres 42 D1
Buckland Gro 49 E1
Buckley Rd 9 F5
Buckleys Row 29 F4
Buckmaster Av 35 H1
Bucknall New Rd 21 H5
Bucknall Old Rd 21 H5
Bucknall Rd 22 B6
Buller St 31 H2
Bulstrode St 14 B6
Bunny Hill 35 H2
Bunts La 17 F1
Burford Way 32 D2
Burgess St 20 B1
Burland Rd 12 A4
Burleigh Gro 20 A6
Burlidge Rd 8 D4
Burlington Av 20 B6
Burmarsh Walk 20 D1
Burnett Pl 16 A1
Burnham St 38 D2
Burnhayes Rd 14 C4
Burnley St 21 H3
Burns Row 40 D5
Burnside Clo 46 C3
Burnwood Pl 9 E5
Burrington Dri 43 F6
Burslem Walkway 15 E6
Bursley Way 13 E6
Burt St 40 D5
Burton Cres 22 A2
Burton Pl 21 G5
Bute St 38 D3
Butler St 31 F6
Butterfield Pl 14 B2
Buttermere Clo 14 B5
Butts Grn 23 F2
Buxton Av 27 F2
Buxton St 21 H1
Byatts Gro 38 D5
Bycars La 14 D4
Bycars Rd 14 D5
Bylands Pl 35 F3
Byron St 30 A3
Cadeby Gro 16 D4
Cadman Cres 16 A2
Cairn Clo 23 G6
Caistor Clo 16 D4
Caldbeck Pl 21 H5
Caldew Gro 43 G6
Caledonia Rd 31 E2
California St 38 D4
Calrofold Dri 12 B4
Calvary Cres 33 G4
Calver St 14 A2
Calverley St 39 G5
Calvert Gro 19 F2
Camberwell Gro 43 G5
Camborne Cres 35 E2
*Cambridge Ct, Cambridge Dri 36 A3
Cambridge Dri 36 A3
Camden St 38 B3
Camelot Clo 48 D1
Cammillus Rd 28 C2
Camoys Rd 20 D1
Camp Rd 15 G4
Campbell Rd 37 E3
Campbell Ter 22 A3
Campion Av 30 A1
Canal La 14 A4
Canal Side 49 F5
Canal St 14 A6
Canberra Cres 47 E4
Canning St 38 B2
Cannon St 31 F1
Canterbury Dri 15 F1
Canvey Gro 46 D4
Cape St 21 G4
Capesthorne St 24 D6
Capewell St 39 F3
Capper St 14 B2
Capricorn Way 8 C4
Carberry Way 40 B3
Card St 20 D1
Cardiff Gro 31 G1
Cardigan Gro 43 G4
Cardington Clo 35 E4
Cardway 13 F6
Cardwell St 22 A4
Carina Gdns 15 H5
Carisbrooke Way 43 G6
Carling Gro 38 D2
Carlisle St 45 E1
Carlos Pl 13 F5
Carlton Av, Brown Edge 11 E4
Carlton Av, Tunstall 14 D1
Carlton Av, Westbury Park 35 G4
Carlton Clo 11 E4
Carlton Rd 31 G4
Carlyon Pl 15 H6
Carmount Rd 23 E1
Carnation Clo 40 D1
Caroline Clo 24 D4
Caroline Cres 11 E4
Caroline St 39 E4
Carpenter Rd 38 D4
Carrick Pl 42 D1
Carroll Dri 39 G3
Carron St 39 E2
Carryer Pl 28 D4
Carson St 14 D3
Cartlidge St 30 A3
Cartmel Pl 15 E2
Cartwright St 39 E5
Casewell Rd 21 G1
Caspian Gro 43 F3
Castel Clo 34 C4
Castle Hill Rd 29 F3
Castle Ridge 29 E4
Castle St, Broad Meadow 18 C1
Castle St, Newcastle 29 H3
Castledine Gro 39 G3
Castlefield St 31 E2
Castleton Rd 46 A2
Castleview Gro 8 C3
Catalina Pl 47 E4
Caterham Pl 46 D5
Catherine Rd 9 F4
Catherine St 20 A5
Caton Cres 16 B3
Cauldon Av 19 E1
Cauldon Rd 31 F3
Caulton St 14 D4
Causeley Gdns 23 E6
Causeley Rd 23 E6
Cavendish Gro 35 F4
Cavendish St 21 E6
Caverswall La 47 E2
Caverswall Old Rd 50 D1
Caverswall Rd, Blythe Bridge 50 D2
Caverswall Rd, Weston Coyney 40 C3
Cavour St 30 C1
Cayley Pl 47 E4
Cecil Av 21 F4
Cedar Av 50 E4
Cedar Cres 11 H4
Cedar Gro 38 B4
Cedar Rd 12 A5
Cellarhead Rd 25 G4
Celtic Av 8 C2
Cemetery Av 39 E6
Cemetery Rd, Knutton 28 C1
Cemetery Rd, Shelton 31 E2
Cemetery Rd, Silverdale 28 B4
Cemetery View 39 E6
Cemlyn Av 38 A5
Central Av 22 D5
Central Dri 38 A4
Century St 21 E4
Chadwell Way 33 G3
Chadwick St 39 F5
Chadwyn Dri 17 E3
Chain St 15 G4
Chalfont Grn 33 E2
Challinor Sq 38 B1
Challinor St 14 B2
Chamberlain Av 36 D1
Chamberlain St 31 F2
Chancery La 39 E4
Chantry Rd 29 F6
Chapel Ct 27 H2
Chapel La, Brown Edge 11 E1
Chapel La, Burslem 14 D6
Chapel St, Abbey Hulton 23 E5
Chapel St, Knutton 28 C1
Chapel St, May Bank 19 H6
Chapel St, Moor Green 50 E1
Chapel St, Silverdale 27 H2
Chaplin Rd, Dresden 45 E2
Chaplin Rd, Longton 39 F6
Chapter Walk 22 D4
Charles St, Hanley 21 G6
Charles St, Wolstanton 20 A6
Charlton St 31 E5

Dryberg Way	22 D5	Elizabeth Dri	18 D1	Farmadine	43 E4	Ford St, Hartshill	30 B3	Gibbing St	21 H3
Dryden Rd	20 D2	Elkstone Clo	8 C6	Farman Clo	47 E4	Ford St, Silverdale	27 H2	Gibson Gro	12 B6
Ducal St	14 B6	Ellams Pl	28 C2	Farmer St	39 F5	Forest Clo	34 C4	Gibson Pl	40 B6
Duddell Rd	15 G4	Ellastone Gro	36 D1	Farmers Bank	27 H3	Forest Rd	46 B3	Gibson St	14 B3
Dudley West	46 B2	Elldawn Av	16 B3	Farmborough Dri	47 E4	Forestside Gro	36 D6	Gifford Pl	30 C6
Duesbury Grn	38 D4	Ellerby Rd	44 B2	Farmwood Clo	40 D6	Forge La	20 C6	Gilchrist Pl	21 E1
Duke Pl	28 A3	Ellers Gro	20 B2	Farndale St	14 B2	Forresters Bank	17 F3	Giles Walk	22 A4
Duke St,		Ellgreave St	14 B6	Farne Gro	38 C4	Forrister St	39 F3	Gill Walk	31 F1
Heron Cross	38 B3	Ellington Clo	32 C2	Farnworth Dri	39 H4	Forster St	14 A2	Gilliat Walk	33 F3
Duke St, Newcastle	29 H5	Elliot Dri	24 D4	Farrington Clo	16 B2	Forsythe Rd	39 E1	Gillman Pl	21 G5
Dulverton Av	35 E2	Elliot Rd	38 B1	Faulkner Pl	40 A3	Forum Dri	18 B3	Gilman Av	17 E3
Duncalf Gro	19 G1	Elliott St	30 A2	Fearns Av	13 F4	Fosbrook Pl	30 A4	Gilman St	21 H6
Duncalf St	14 C6	Ellis St	21 F1	Fearson Grn	16 A2	Foundry La	32 D1	Gimson St	21 G5
Duncan St	32 A6	Ellison St	20 A3	Featherstone Gro	30 D5	Foundry Sq	10 C6	Girsby Clo	48 D1
Dundas St	21 H4	Elm Pl	38 C6	Federation Rd	14 C5	Foundry St	21 G5	Gitana St	21 G5
Dundee Rd	30 D1	Elm St, Cobridge	21 E2	Fegg Hayes Rd	8 D4	Fountain Sq	14 C6	Gladstone Pl	36 C2
Dundee St	38 D6	Elm St, Wolstanton	30 A1	Fell St	15 G4	Fountain St	38 A1	Gladstone St	30 B2
Dunkirk	29 F3	Elmbrook Clo	46 A3	Fellbrook La	22 D5	Fountains Av	35 F3	Gladwyn St	23 F5
Dunkirk Ct	29 F3	Elmcroft Rd	23 E3	Felstead St	17 E2	Fourth Av	23 H5	Glaisher Dri	47 E4
Dunning St	14 A1	Elmdon Pl	46 D3	Fenlow Av	32 C2	Fowlers La	17 G4	Glandore Rd	40 B3
Dunrobin St	39 F6	Elmhurst Clo	32 C2	Fennel Gro	46 C5	Fox Gro	35 H6	Glass St	21 G5
Dunsany Gro	22 A2	Elms Way	40 C6	Fenpark Rd	38 C1	Foxfield Way	44 B2	Glastonbury Clo	16 G2
Dunsford Av	16 D4	Elmsmere Av	44 C1	Fenton Park	32 D6	Foxglove Clo	40 D2	Glebe Clo	50 E3
Dunster Rd	39 E2	Elmsmere Rd	23 E2	Fenton Rd	32 B2	Foxglove Gro	35 H6	Glebe Ct	31 F5
Dunwood Dri	15 E2	Elmstead Clo	42 C2	Fermain Clo	34 D4	Foxlands Clo	23 G6	Glebe St	31 F5
Durber Clo	36 B3	Elmwood Clo	50 E3	Fern Pl	39 E6	Foxley La	16 C5	Glebedale Rd	38 A1
Durham Gro	36 A3	Elmwood Dri	50 E3	Ferncroft	43 E4	Frampton Gro	8 C4	Glencastle Way	43 G6
Durston Pl	40 A5	Elphinstone Rd	36 C4	Ferndale Clo,		Francis St	8 C5	Glencoe St	38 D6
Dyke St	21 H5	Elsby Pl	9 E4	Blythe Bridge	50 D4	Frank St	37 E1	Glendale St	14 D6
Dylan Rd	39 G4	Elsing St	37 H1	Ferndale Clo,		Franklin Rd	30 C6	Glendue Gro	43 G5
		Elstree Clo	40 B6	Washerwall	24 C4	Franklyn St	31 H1	Gleneagles Cres	22 A2
Eagle St	22 A5	Elswick Rd	32 A4	Ferndown Clo	45 G2	Fraser St	21 F1	Glenfield Way	33 H5
Eamont Av	15 E1	Eltham Gdns	20 B6	Ferndown Dri Sth	34 B5	Freckleton Pl	47 E4	Glenroyd Av	32 D2
Eardly St	36 D1	Ely Walk	39 F3	Ferndown Rd	35 H6	Frederick Av	30 D5	Glenroyd Walk	33 F3
Earl St, Newcastle	29 H3	Embelton Walk	20 B1	Fernhurst Gro	46 A3	Frederick St	32 B6	Glenwood Clo, Longton	39 E3
Earl St, Silverdale	27 H3	Emberton St,		Fernlea Gro,		Freehold St	29 H5	Glenwood Clo,
Earls Ct	29 H3	Broad Meadow	18 C2	Meir Heath	45 G5	Freetraders St	21 H4	Silverdale	27 H3
Earls Dri	35 G1	Emberton St, Dimsdale	19 H3	Fernlea Gro,		Fremantle Rd	36 C3	Globe St	14 B6
Earls Rd	43 F4	Emerson Rd	20 D2	Weston Coyney	40 D2	Frenchmoor Gro	45 H1	Gloucester Grange	35 H3
Earlsbrook Dri	43 F3	Emery Av, Newcastle	29 E5	Fernwood Grn	43 G4	Friar St	39 F3	Glover St	21 H3
Easdale St	35 G2	Emery Av,		Ferrand Clo	36 D6	Friars Pl	23 E1	Glyn Pl	14 D2
Easedale Clo	16 D4	Sneyd Green	16 A6	Festing St	21 H4	Friars Rd	23 E1	Gobden St	45 E1
East Bank Ride	50 E1	Emery St	21 E3	Festival Way	20 C4	Friars St	29 G4	Goddard St	39 F4
East Cres	30 A1	Empire St	37 E1	Fiddlers La	11 E1	Friars Walk	35 G1	Godfrey Rd	23 E6
East Grn	46 B1	Emsworth Rd	44 A2	Field Av	17 E4	Friarswood Rd	29 F4	Golborn Av	45 F5
East Precincts	21 G6	Encounter Pl	22 B4	Field Clo	47 H5	Frobisher St	10 C6	Golborn Clo	45 G5
East St	40 D2	Enderley St	29 F2	Field Pl	39 F2	Frodingham Rd	33 H3	Gold St	39 E4
East Ter	9 F4	Endon Rd,		Field View	40 D4	Froghall	29 F3	Goldenhill Rd	39 E3
East View	20 C1	Norton Green	10 C5	Fielden Clo	16 B3	Frome Walk	8 D6	Goldsmith Pl	39 G3
Eastbank Rd	21 E4	Endon Rd, Norton		Fieldend Clo	43 F4	Fuller St	14 B1	Goms Mill Rd	38 C6
Eastbourne Rd	22 A5	in the Moors	16 B1	Fielding St	37 F2	Fulmar Pl	46 D4	Goodfellow St	14 A1
Eastbridge Av	15 H6	Englesea Av	40 C2	Fieldway, Ash Bank	24 B5	Fulwood Walk	33 F3	Goodson St	21 G5
Eastdean Av	32 C2	Ennerdale Clo	14 B6	Fieldway,		Furlong La	14 C6	Goodwick Clo	43 G6
Easter Rd	16 D5	Enoch St	14 D6	Blythe Bridge	47 F3	Furlong Par	14 C6	Goodwin Av	29 F1
Easthead Walk	31 E1	Enstone Clo	44 B2	Fieldway, Hollybush	38 B5	Furlong Rd	8 B6	Goodwin Rd	40 D5
Eastwick Cres	42 D2	Enstone Ct	35 F5	Fife St	38 D3	Furlong View	14 C6	Goodwood Pl	43 E4
Eastwood Av	15 E1	Ephraim St	31 G1	Filey Clo	33 G2	Furnace Rd	39 G6	Goose St	29 G4
Eastwood Pl	31 G1	Epping Rd	36 B4	Finchdean Clo	46 C4	Furnival St	21 F2	Gordon Av	21 G1
Eastwood Rd	31 H1	Epworth St	31 E6	Finchsmith Pl	38 D5			Gordon Cres	22 A2
Eaton St	21 H5	Ernest Pl	32 B6	Finney Grn	22 C6	Gable St	37 F1	Gordon St, Knutton	28 C1
Eaves La	23 F4	Eros Cres	22 B2	Finstock Av	44 A3	Gainsborough Rd,		Gordon St, Smallthorn	15 E4
Eaveswood Rd	23 F3	Errill Clo	31 G6	Fir Tree Pl	12 C5	Blurton	44 B2	Gorse St	38 B3
Ebor St	39 G6	Erskine St	39 F6	First Av, Porthill	19 H1	Gainsborough Rd,		Gort Rd	18 D6
Ebury Gro	46 A1	Esk Walk	35 G3	First Av, Townsend	23 G6	Broad Meadow	18 C3	Gosfirth Gro	47 E3
Ecclestone Pl	9 E4	Eskdale Pl, Clayton	35 G1	Firtree Rd	45 H2	Galloway Rd	33 H4	Govan Rd	32 B4
Edale Clo	27 G3	Eskdale Pl, Trentham	42 D4	Fishpond Way	22 D2	Gallowstree La	28 C5	Gowan Av	8 D6
Eddisbury Dri	12 A3	Esperanto Way	15 G5	Fistral Clo	39 G4	Galsworthy Rd	39 E1	Gower St, Longton	39 F5
Eden Gro	46 B1	Essex Pl	35 E1	Fitzgerald Clo	40 D3	Garden Pl	30 B5	Gower St,
Edensor Ct	12 C6	Eton Av	34 D3	Fitzherbert Rd	16 B6	Garden St, Newcastle	29 G4	The Brampton	29 H3
Edensor Rd	39 E5	Etruria Old Rd	30 C1	Five Oaks Clo	34 D4	Garden St, Penkhull	36 C1	Grafton Av	15 F4
Edensor St	12 C6	Etruria Rd, Basford	30 A2	Fixdale Clo	21 G4	Gardenholm Clo	46 A3	Grafton Rd	39 E3
Edensor Ter	38 D5	Etruria Rd, Etruria	20 C6	Flackett St	39 E3	Gardiner Dri	38 D5	Grafton St	21 H4
Edgar Pl	39 F1	Etruscan St	30 C1	Flamborough Gro	14 B6	Garfield Av	42 D2	Graham St	22 C6
Edge Av	8 D4	Etruscan Walk	49 H1	Flash La,		Garfield Rd	14 B6	Granby Walk	30 D6
Edge La	11 G3	Evans St	14 C4	Baddeley Edge	17 F3	Garfield Cres	42 D2	Grange La	20 A5
Edge St	14 C4	Evelyn St	38 A1	Flash La,		Garibaldi St	31 E1	Grange Rd	46 B4
Edge View Rd	17 F3	Eversley Rd	39 H6	Trent Vale	36 C4	Garlick St	15 F5	Grange St	21 E2
Edgefield Rd	39 F2	Evesham Way	39 H4	Flatts Rd	10 A6	Garner St	30 C1	Grangemore Ter	20 A6
Edgefields La	11 F5	Exeter St	33 F2	Flax St	37 E1	Garner St	21 E6	Grangewood Av	46 B2
Edgeview Clo	17 E3	Exmore Gro	21 E1	Flaxman Clo	49 G1	Garnett Rd East	19 G3	Grangewood Rd	46 B2
Edgware St	21 E3	Eyre St	20 B1	Fleckney Av	39 H4	Garnett Rd West	19 G3	Granstone Clo	33 F3
Edison St	37 H1			Fleming St	31 E6	Garnham Pl	39 E5	Grant St	31 G6
Edmonton Gro	16 C5	Faceby Gro	47 E4	Fletcher Bank	29 F3	Garsdale Cres	44 B2	Grantchester Clo	46 D5
Ednam Pl	46 B2	Fairbank Av	36 D3	Fletcher Cres	17 E4	Garth St	21 H5	Grantham Pl	22 D3
Edwal Rd	40 C3	Fairbank Pl	40 B3	Fletcher Rd	37 E2	Gaskell Rd	23 G6	Grantley Clo	44 D1
Edward Av,		Fairclough Pl	14 D2	Fletcher St	31 F1	Gate St	40 D2	Granville Av,
Hem Heath	43 F4	Faircroft Av	18 D2	Fleur Gro	39 E1	Gate Way	12 B3	Sneyd Green	21 H1
Edward St, Newcastle	35 G1	Fairfax St	21 H3	Flint St	40 D2	Gatley Gro	46 D5	Granville Av,
Edward Davies Rd	15 G3	Fairfield Av,		Flintsham Gro	21 G4	Gawsworth Clo	39 G1	The Brampton	29 H2
Edward St, Fenton	32 A6	Brown Edge	11 E3	Florence Rd	36 D6	Gayton Av	16 D4	Granville Rd	23 E4
Edward St, Dimsdale	19 H5	Fairfield Av, Dimsdale	19 H5	Florence St	29 G3	Gedney Gro	35 G6	Granville St	21 F3
Edward St, Wolstanton	20 A5	Fairfield Av, Florence	45 F2	Florida St	15 E6	Geen St	31 E5	Grasmere Av	35 G3
Egerton Rd	30 B4	Fairhaven Gro	22 A2	Floyd St	31 E5	Gemini Gro	8 C4	Grasmere Ter	15 E2
Egerton St	31 H3	Fairlawn Clo	46 A3	Foden St	37 E2	Geneva Dri, Hanley	22 B2	Gratton Rd	23 G6
Elaine Av	15 F4	Fairlawns	29 G1	Fogg St	29 G3	Geneva Dri, Westlands	28 C6	Gravelly Bank	46 A3
Elburton Rd	32 D6	Fairlight Gro	46 C4	Foley Pl	38 D3	Geoffrey Gro	40 C3	Grayshott Rd	8 B3
Elder Pl	21 E2	Fairway	42 B3	Foley Rd	38 D4	George Av	46 C1	Greasley Rd	22 D3
Elder Rd	21 E3	Fairway Rd	15 E2	Foley St	38 D3	George Ct	39 E4	Greatbatch Av	36 C1
Eldon St	21 H3	Falkirk Grange	28 D5	Fontaine Pl	37 E2	George St, Chesterton	18 C1	Green Clo, Barlaston	49 E5
Eleanor Cres	35 F1	Fallowfield	44 B2	Fonthill Walk	22 D5	George St, Dimsdale	19 H3	Green Clo,
Eleanor Pl	29 F6	Faraday Pl	30 B5	Forber St	36 C3	George St, Fenton	32 A6	Blythe Bridge	47 F4
Eleanor View	35 F1	Fareham Gro	46 A3	Ford Av	9 E5	George St, Newcastle	29 H4	Green La	50 D3
Elenora St	31 E5	Farington Pl	9 E4	Ford Green Rd	15 G4	George St, Silverdale	27 G2	Green Rd	36 B4
Elgar Cres	22 C3	Farland St	8 D4	Ford Hayes La	33 G4	Gerrard St	31 E4	Greenacres	47 F3
Elgin St	31 E3	Farleigh Gro	33 E2						

Greenbank Gro 19 H5
Greenbank Rd 14 C2
Greendock St 38 D4
Greenfield Av 11 F3
Greenfield Clo 11 F3
Greenfield Pl 11 F3
Greenfield Rd 8 B6
Greengates St 14 B1
Greenhead St 14 C5
Greenhill Rd 10 A5
Greenlea Clo 43 G6
Greenmeadow Gro 11 H5
Greenmore Av 8 D2
Greenock Clo 28 D5
Greens La 33 H1
Greenside 29 F3
Greenside Av 17 F2
Greenway 38 A5
Greenway Av 15 F3
Greenway Bank 17 F3
Greenway Hall Rd 16 G2
Greenway Pl 23 E1
Greenwood Av 36 B5
Greenwood Rd 50 E1
Greeting St 20 D1
Gregory St 38 D4
Gregson Clo 38 C5
Grenadier Clo 49 E1
Grendon Grn 33 F2
Greville St 21 H4
Greyfriars Rd 22 D4
Greyling Gro 15 F2
Greysan Av 8 C2
Greyswood Rd 36 B4
Grice Rd 30 B4
Griffin St 38 D4
Grindley La 46 B6
Grindley Pl 30 C6
Grisdale Clo 46 C3
Gristhorpe Way 33 H3
Gritton St 14 B3
Grosvenor Av 36 C3
Grosvenor Gdns 29 H4
Grosvenor Pl, Dimsdale 19 H4
Grosvenor Pl, Tunstall 14 A1
Grosvenor Rd, Meir 46 A1
Grosvenor Rd,
Newcastle 29 G4
Grosvenor St 38 D4
Grove Av 38 A3
Grove Pl 31 F1
Grove Rd 37 G2
Grove St, Cobridge 21 E2
Grove St, Knutton 28 C1
Grovebank Rd 36 B4
Guernsey Dri 34 C4
Guernsey Walk 38 C4
Guildford St 31 G4
Guy St 23 E5
Gwenys Cres 38 A4

Hackett Clo 39 F4
Hackwood Clo 49 H1
Hadden Clo 24 C6
Haddon Gro 18 D2
Haddon Pl 23 E4
Hadleigh Gro 35 G6
Hadleigh Rd 23 E2
Hadrian Way 18 B3
Haggett Gro 39 F6
Haig St 39 G5
Hailsham Clo 8 C6
Hales Pl 45 F1
Halesworth Cres 35 G6
Halfway Pl 28 C2
Halifax Clo 47 E4
Hall Dri 40 D3
Hall Hill Dri 33 G4
Hall Pl 20 A3
Hall St, Burslem 14 C6
Hall St, Newcastle 29 F3
Hallahan Gro 30 D4
Hallam St 38 A1
Halldearn Av 41 F4
Hallfield Gro 8 B6
Halton Grn 44 A2
Hamble Way 33 G3
Hambro Pl 9 F3
Hamill Rd 14 D5
Hamilton Rise 16 D3
Hamilton Road 39 G6
Hamilton St 37 G2
Hamlet Pl 16 B2
Hammersley St 22 A3
Hammerton Av 32 C2
Hammond Av 11 E3
Hammond Rd 12 D6
Hammoon Gro 33 E1
Hamner Grn 33 G4
Hampstead Gro 43 G4
Hampton St 31 H2
Hanbridge Av 19 E2
Hancock St 31 G5
Hand St 14 B3
Handley Banks 41 H2
Hanley Rd 15 G5
Hanover St, Hanley 21 F4
Hanover St, Newcastle 29 G3
Harber St 39 F4
Harcourt Av 46 B1
Harcourt St 31 F2
Hardewick Clo 24 D6
Harding Rd 31 G2
Harding Ter 36 D1
Hardinge St 31 H6
Hardman St 16 C5
Hardsacre Rd 39 G2
Hardtree Walk 36 D6
Hardwick Clo 48 D1
Hardy St 8 A6
Hareshaw Gro 9 E2
Harewood St 14 A3
Hargreave Clo 47 F4
Harington Dri 39 H2
Harlech Av 45 H2
Harlequin Av 15 G3
Harley St 21 G6
Harold St 15 G5
Harper Av 19 F5
Harper St 14 B6
Harpfield Rd 36 B1
Harris St 30 D5
Harrison Rd 16 B3
Harrison St 29 H5
Harrogate Gro 27 E1
Harrop St 22 A3
Harrowby Dri 35 E3
Harrowby Rd 46 B3
Hart Ct 29 F3
Harthill St 31 G5
Hartington St 19 F3
Hartland Av 15 G1
Hartshill Rd 30 A3
Hartwell La, Barlaston 49 H5
Hartwell La,
Rough Close 45 E6
Hartwell Rd 46 C2
Harvey Rd 40 C6
Hassal St 21 H6
Hassam Av 29 F1
Hassam Par 19 F3
Hassell St 29 G4
Hatfield Cres 44 A2
Hathersage Clo 39 F1
Hatherton Clo 12 A4
Hatrell St 29 G5
Havelet Dri 34 D4
Havelock Pl 31 E2
Haven Av 15 H5
Haven Cres 24 D4
Haven Gro 19 G1
Hawes St 14 A1
Hawkesdale Clo 46 C4
Hawkins St 37 G1
Hawkstone Clo 29 H5
Hawthorn Pl 46 B2
Hawthorn St 21 E2
Hawthorne Av 36 B2
Hawthorne Rd 12 C4
Hay Mkt 14 A2
Haydon St 30 B2
Hayes St 15 G3
Hayfield Cres 32 A5
Hayfield Rd 27 G3
Hayling Pl 38 C5
Hayner Gro 40 D3
Haywood Rd 14 D3
Haywood St 31 F3
Hazel Clo 36 C2
Hazel Gro 40 B6
Hazel Rd 12 B5
Hazeldene Rd 43 F4
Hazelhurst Rd 8 D5
Hazelhurst St 31 H1
Hazelwood Rd 11 H4
Hazlemere Av 17 E4
Hazlitt Way 39 H2
Heakley Av 16 B1
Healey Pl 39 F5
Heanor Pl 38 D4
Heath Av, Cellarhead 25 G4
Heath Av,
May Bank 19 G6
Heath Gro 45 G5
Heath House La 22 C5
Heath Pass 39 G5
Heath Pl 19 G6
Heath St,
Broad Meadow 18 D3
Heath St, Newcastle 29 G3
Heathcote Av 31 E5
Heathcote Rise 40 D3
Heathcote Road 38 D4
Heathcote St, Crackley 12 C6
Heathcote St,
Sandford Hill 39 E1
Heathdene Clo 39 E3
Heather Clo 24 C4
Heather Cres 45 G5
Heather Hills 11 G5
Heatherlands Clo 45 F5
Heatherleigh Gro 22 B3
Heathfield Gro 46 B5
Heathfield Rd,
Chell Heath 9 G6
Heathfield Rd, Crackley 12 B4
Heaton Ter 19 G2
Heber St 39 F3
Hedley Pl 29 E4
Helena St 32 B6
Helston Av 39 H4
Heming Pl 22 C6
Hemingway Rd 39 G3
Hempstalls Gro 19 G6
Hempstalls La 29 G2
Hemsby Way 35 F5
Henderson Gro 40 D5
Henley Clo 49 G1
Henry St 14 A1
Henshall Rd 12 D6
Herbert Rd 39 G6
Herbert St 31 H6
Herd St 14 C4
Hereford Av 35 G3
Hereford Gro 33 G2
Herm Clo 34 C3
Hermes Clo 47 E4
Heron St 38 A2
Hertford Gro 35 H4
Hertford St 38 B3
Hesketh Av 10 A5
Heskin Way 9 E4
Hester Clo 33 F6
Hethersett Walk 33 G2
Hewitt Cres 24 C5
Hewitt St 8 D4
Heyburn Cres 14 B5
Heysham Clo 40 D3
Hickman St 29 F3
Hide St 31 E6
High Bank Pl 15 F4
High La,
Brown Edge 10 D5
High La,
Great Chell 8 D4
High St, Caverswall 41 G5
High St, Crackley 18 C1
High St, Knutton 28 C1
High St, Newcastle 29 G3
High St, Porthill 19 H2
High St, Sandyford 8 A6
High St, Silverdale 27 F2
High St, Tunstall 14 B2
High View 45 F5
Highcroft Walk 15 F4
Higherland 29 E4
Highfield Av, Meir 46 A1
Highfield Av,
Wolstanton 20 A5
Highfield Clo 47 F4
Highfield Ct 35 G1
Highfield Dri 38 A4
Highfield Grange 20 B6
Highgrove Rd 36 C4
Highland Clo 47 H4
Highton St 17 E5
Highville Pl 36 D2
Highway La 26 B6
Higson Av 31 E5
Hilderstone Rd 45 F5
Hill St 31 E5
Hill Top Cres 45 F5
Hill View 17 E3
Hilland Clo 27 G3
Hillary St 21 F2
Hillberry Clo 32 D2
Hillchurch St 21 G5
Hillcrest St 21 H5
Hillfield Av 36 B3
Hillgreen Rd 39 G1
Hillman St 17 E5
Hillport Av 19 F1
Hillside 29 E5
Hillside Av, Forsbrook 50 E2
Hillside Av, Meir 46 A1
Hillside Clo 17 F3
Hillside Rd,
Baddeley Edge 17 F3
Hillside Rd, Washerwall 24 C4
Hillside Walk 30 A4
Hillswood Dri 11 H2
Hilltop Av 30 B1
Hilton Rd 30 B6
Hincho Pl 10 A6
Hinckley Gro 43 F6
Hines St 38 A2
Hinton Clo 44 C2
Hitchman St 38 A1
Hobart St 21 E1
Hobson St 15 E6
Hodgkinson St 18 D2
Hodnet Gro 21 F3
Hogarth Pl 18 C2
Holbeach Av 32 C2
Holborn 29 F3
Holbrook Walk 33 E2
Holdcroft Rd 23 E4
Holden Av 20 A6
Holden Avenue Nth 15 H6
Holden Avenue Sth 15 H6
Holditch Rd 18 D4
Holehouse Rd 23 E3
Holland St 14 A1
Hollies Dri 45 F5
Hollings St 38 D2
Hollington Dri 9 E2
Hollinshead Av 19 F5
Hollowood Pl 10 A6
Hollowood Walk 10 A6
Holly Dri 24 C5
Holly Pl 38 B3
Holly Rd 12 B5
Hollybank Cres 36 D3
Hollybush Rd 38 A4
Hollywood La 26 B3
Holmes Way 9 F2
Holmesfield Walk 39 G4
Holst Dri 22 C3
Holybush Cres 38 A4
Holyhead Cres 40 D3
Homer Pl 9 F5
Homer St 22 A6
Homestead St 33 H4
Honeysuckle Av 50 D4
Honeywall 30 D6
Honeywood 29 G1
Honiton Walk 39 G4
Hoon Av 19 G5
Hoover St 14 A2
Hope St 21 F4
Hopedale Clo,
Sandford Hill 33 E6
Hopedale Clo,
Westbury Park 35 G5
Hopton Way 9 E2
Hopwood Pl 23 E6
Horatius Rd 18 B3
Hordley St 21 H5
Hornby Row 31 E6
Horsley Gro 44 A2
Horton Dri 40 C2
Horton St 30 A3
Horwood Gdns 15 G5
Hose St 14 A2
Hoskins Rd 8 B6
Hot La 15 E6
Hough Hill 11 E1
Houghton St 31 G1
Houghwood La 17 H1
Houldsworth Dri 9 E3
Housefield Rd 33 G4
Houseman Dri 40 A3
Hoveringham Dri 32 B2
Howard Clo 24 C4
Howard Gro 29 E6
Howard Pl, Newcastle 29 E6
Howard Pl, Shelton 31 F2
Howard St 39 E6
Howe Gro 28 C2
Howson St 31 H1
Hudson Walk 39 F4
Hughes Av 29 F1
Hughes St 21 E1
Hulme Clo 27 H3
Hulme La 24 C6
Hulme Rd 40 A2
Hulme St 30 C4
Hulse St 38 D1
Hulton Rd 23 E3
Hulton St 21 H4
Humber St 30 D1
Humber Way 35 F4
Hunt St 14 B2
Huntbach St 21 G5
Hunters Dri 36 D1
Hunters Way 36 D1
Huntilee Rd 14 C2
Huntingdon Pl 22 C2
Huntley Av 36 D1
Huntsbank Dri 12 B4
Huron Gro 43 E3
Hurst St 38 D4
Hutchinson Walk 38 C5
Hutton Way 33 G2
Huxley Pl 39 G4
Hyacinth Ct 29 G1
Hyndley Clo 32 D1

Ibsen Rd 40 B3
Ilam Clo 27 G3
Ilford Side 44 B2
Ilkley Pl 27 E2
Imandra Clo 43 E3
Imogen Clo 39 E1
INDUSTRIAL ESTATES:
Brampton Ind Est 29 F2
Cinderhill Ind Est 40 A4
Far Green Ind Est 21 H3
Fen Park Ind Est 38 C2
Hamilton Ind Est 38 A1
Holditch Ind Est 19 E4
Lomer Rd Ind Est 18 C3
Longbridge Hayes
Ind Est 13 F4
Longport Enterprise
Centre 14 A6
Newstead Trading Est 43 H4
Parkhouse Ind Est
East 13 E4
Parkhouse Ind Est
West 12 D6
Scott Lidgett Ind Est 20 A1
Sneyd Trading Est 15 F5
Stonewalk Ind Est 28 B2
Wolstanton Retail
Park 20 B5
Ingelow Clo 38 D6
Ingestre Sq 44 B2
Ingleborough Pl 17 G5
Inglefield Av 15 F4
Ingleton Gro 46 C3
Inglewood Dri 19 H2
Inglewood Gro 19 H2
Inglis St 31 G5
Intake Rd 10 A6
Iona Pl 38 C5
Ipswick Walk 33 E1
Irene Av, Basford 30 A1
Irene Av, Tunstall 14 D2
Iris Clo 41 E2
Ironmarket 29 G3
Islay Walk 38 C5
Ivy Clo 50 D3
Ivy Gro 42 C2
Ivy House Rd 22 A6
Ivyhouse Dri 49 G1

Jack Ashley Ct 38 A1
Jack Haye La 17 G5
Jackfield St 15 E4
Jackson St 14 D5
Jacqueline St 13 H1
Jade Ct 39 G3
Jamage Rd 12 B1
James Cres 25 E4
James St, Boothen 36 C2
James St, Dimsdale 19 H3
Janet Pl 22 A4
Janson St 42 C1
Jasmine Clo 50 D3
Jason St 29 F2
Jasper Clo 49 H1
Jasper St 31 G1
Java Cres 43 F3
Jaycean Av 8 B6
Jean Clo 14 D3
Jefferson St 14 A1
Jenkins St 14 D5
Jenkinson Clo 29 E5
Jerbourg Clo 34 C4
Jeremy Clo 36 D1
Jersey Clo 34 C3
Jervis St 21 H4
Jervison St 39 G1
Jesmond Gro 44 A3
Joanhurst Cres 31 E1
John Bright St 21 H4
John St, Crackley 12 C6
John St, Hanley 21 G6
John St, Knutton 28 D1
John St, Newcastle 30 A3
Johns Sq 14 C6
Johnson Av 19 E5
Johnson Pl 9 E4
Johnson St 18 B1
Johnstone Av 25 E4
Jolley St 15 G4
Jolyon Clo 39 E1
Jonathan Rd 43 G6
Jordan St 31 E1
Joseph St 14 C6
Josiah Wedgwood St 21 E6
Joyce Av 15 F3
Jubilee Av 31 E1
Jubilee Rd, Trentham 42 C2
Jubilee Rd, Wolstanton 20 A6
Judith Gro 37 G3
June Rd 39 E1
Juniper Clo 46 C5
Jupiter St 15 G4
Justin Clo 20 A2

Kara Pl 43 F3
Kartley St 15 G3
Kaydor Clo 24 D4
Kearsley Way 44 A2
Keary St 37 E1
Keble Way 38 C6
Kedleston Rd 15 E4
Keele By-Pass 26 C4
Keele Rd 26 A4

Piccadilly 21 G6
Piccadilly St 14 A2
Pickering Clo 44 D1
Pickford Pl 46 B1
Pickmere Clo 17 E2
Picton St 21 H6
Pidduck St 20 B1
Pierce St 14 A2
Piggott Grn 22 D6
Pilkington Av 35 F1
Pilsbury St 20 A3
Pilsden Pl 47 E4
Pine Ct 47 F3
Pine Rd 37 G3
Pinehurst Clo 35 F5
Pinetree Dri 47 F3
Pinewood Cres 40 D6
Pinewood Gro, Crackley 12 C5
Pinewood Gro, Forsbrook 50 E3
Pinfold Av 16 A1
Pinhoe Pl 39 H4
Pinnox St 14 B3
Pireford Pl 13 F4
Pirehill Rd 13 F5
Pitcairn St 14 B2
Pitfield Av 20 A6
Pitgreen La 20 A3
Pitsford St 39 H5
Pitt St East 14 D6
Pitts Hill Bank 8 C6
Plainfield Gro 33 G4
Plane Gro 12 C5
Plant St 39 F3
Plantation Rd 43 H4
Platts Av 11 H4
Pleasant St 20 C1
Plex St 14 A2
Pleydell St 16 B6
Plough St 21 H4
Plumtree Gro 22 C2
Plymouth Gro 18 D1
Pochard Clo 15 G3
Podmore St 21 E1
Pointon Gro 10 C5
Polperro Walk 46 C4
Pool Dam 29 F4
Pool St, Newcastle 29 F4
Pool St, Sandford Hill 38 D1
Poole Av 17 E3
Poolfield Av 29 E4
Poolfields Clo 28 D4
Poolside, Newcastle 29 F3
Poolside, Blurton 44 B2
Poplar Av 19 E6
Poplar Clo, Blythe Bridge 50 D3
Poplar Clo, Cross Heath 19 E6
Poplar Ct 19 F6
Poplar Dri 38 B6
Poplar Gro, Blurton 44 C1
Poplar Gro, Newcastle 29 H3
Porlock Gro 43 F5
Port St 20 B1
Port Vale St 14 B6
Porthill 19 H2
Porthill Grange 19 H2
Porthill Grn 19 H2
Porthill Rd 20 A1
Portland Clo 47 F4
Portland Cres 50 F1
Portland Gro 35 G4
Portland Pl 49 H1
Portland Rd 39 E3
Portland St 21 F4
Potteries Way 21 F4
Poulson St 31 E6
Pound Gdns 15 H1
Poundgate Clo 43 E3
Povey Pl 13 F5
Povey St 14 C6
Powderham Clo 8 B2
Powell St 21 E4
Power Gro 38 D4
Prestbury Av 35 G6
Preston St 15 G5
Pretoria Rd 30 D1
Priam Clo 13 F5
Price St 14 D5
Priestley Dri 39 G3
Prime St 22 A4
Primitive St 15 H4
Primrose Gro 29 G1
Primrose Hill 37 E6
Princes Rd 30 C4
Princess Dri 40 C4
Princess Sq 14 A6
Princess St, Newcastle 29 H3
Princess St, Tunstall 14 A3
Priorfield Clo 39 E3
Priory Rd, Abbey Hulton 23 E2
Priory Rd, Newcastle 29 F6
Prospect Pl 36 C4
Prospect St 20 B2
Prospect Ter 29 F3
Providence St 21 H3
Pump Bank 27 E5
Pump St 31 E5
Purbeck St 21 F2
Purser Cres 19 G4
Pyenest St 31 E2

Quadrant Rd 21 G5
Quarry Av 30 D4
Quarry Bank Rd 27 E4
Quarry Clo, Baddeley Edge 17 F2
Quarry Clo, Washerwall 24 C4
Quarry Rd 30 D5
Queen Anne St 31 F4
Queen Ct 29 G3
*Queen Elizabeth Ct, Temple St 37 H1
Queen Mary Rd 36 D6
Queen Marys Dri 49 G2
Queen St, Burslem 14 C6
Queen St, Chesterton 18 C1
Queen St, Newcastle 29 G3
Queen St, Porthill 19 G2
Queens Av 14 C2
Queens Ct 22 A5
Queens Park Av 44 D1
Queens Rd 30 C5
Queens Row 49 H4
Queens Walk 40 C4
Queens Way 35 F1
Queensbury Rd 39 G6
Queensmead Rd 46 A3
Queensway, Boothen 37 F3
Queensway, Etruria 30 B1
Quintin Walk 15 G3
Quinton Gro 19 G5

Race Course 28 A3
Racecourse Rd 36 D3
Rachel Gro 39 E1
Radford Rd 30 C3
Radley Way 24 D4
Radstone Rise 35 F5
Raglan St 37 H1
Raglan Walk 37 H1
Railton Av 44 C1
Railway Pass 39 F4
Railway Rd 40 A5
Railway St 14 B3
Railway Ter 39 G4
Rainham Gro 9 E1
Ralph Dri 16 B6
Ramage Gro 45 G1
Ramsey Clo 49 G1
Ramsey Rd 29 E1
Ramsey St 37 G2
Ramshaw Gro 39 G1
Ranelagh St 21 G6
Ransome Pl 40 A3
Ranworth Clo 35 F6
Rathbone Av 20 A6
Rathbone St 14 B2
Rattigan Dri 40 B3
Ratton St 21 H5
Ravenswood Clo 35 F4
Rawlins St 22 A4
Rayleigh Way 33 G3
Raymond Av 21 H1
Raymond St 31 F1
Reading Way 33 G1
Rebecca St 31 E5
Recorder Grn 9 F4
Recreation Rd 39 H6
Rectory Pass 31 F1
Rectory Rd 31 E2
Rectory St 31 E1
Red House Cres 38 D4
Red La 17 F4
Red Lion Pass 31 F1
Redbridge Clo 42 C1
Redcar Rd 43 E3
Redheath Clo 27 E2
Redhills Rd 16 C6
Redlands Dri 23 G6
Redman Gro 21 G1
Redmine Clo 19 E4
Redwood Pl 46 B1
Reedbed Gro 15 G2
Reedham Way 33 G2
Reeves Av, Bank Top 15 E2
Reeves Av, May Bank 19 F6
*Refinery St, Stubbs Gate 29 G4
Regent Av 14 C2
Regent Ct 19 G2
Regent Rd 31 G1
Regent St 36 D2
Regina St 15 H3
Reginald St 14 D5
Registry St 31 F5
Remer St 21 E3
Renfrew Clo 28 D5
Renfrew Pl 42 D1
Renown Clo 32 C3
Repington Rd 16 B6
Repton Dri 34 D2
Reservoir Rd 39 H6
Reynard Walk 46 D4
Reynolds Av 18 C2
Reynolds Rd 14 D2
Rhodes Ct 19 H2
Rhodes St 21 H3
Rhondda Av 21 G1
Ribble Clo 35 F4
Ricardo St 45 E1
Riceyman Rd 13 F5
Richards Av 14 C2
Richardson Pl 9 F4
Richmond Av 15 H6
Richmond Gro 30 B1
Richmond Rd 42 D1
Richmond St 30 D4
Richmond Ter 31 F2
Ridge Clo 49 E6
Ridge Cres 46 B5
Ridge Walk 46 A3
Ridgehouse Dri 20 C4
Ridgeway Rd 31 G3
Ridgmont Rd 34 D4
Ridgway Dri 47 F4
Ridgway Pl 20 A3
Ridley St 37 G2
Ried St 14 B6
Riley Av 15 F3
Riley St Nth 14 C6
Riley St Sth 14 C6
Rill St 39 E3
Ringland Clo 21 H5
Ripon Av 18 C1
Rippon Rd 44 B3
Riseley Rd 30 B4
Rists Rd 19 E5
Rithin Rd 33 F1
Riverhead Clo 10 C6
Riverside Rd 36 B5
Rivington Cres 9 E4
Robert Heath St 15 G4
Robert St 14 A1
Roberts Av 29 F1
Robertson Dri 18 D6
Robertson Sq 36 C3
Robin Croft 14 D6
Robin Hill Gro 39 E2
Robinson Av 15 H6
Robinson Ct 44 B2
Robinson Rd 42 C3
Robson St 21 F6
Rochester Rd 39 E2
Rochford Way 33 G2
Rock House Dri 49 F5
Rockfield Av 17 G4
Roe La 35 E3
Roebuck St 31 G5
Rogate Clo 39 E1
Rogers Av 18 D6
Rogerston Av 30 B6
Rolfe Clo 36 D6
Roman Dri 18 B3
Romer Side 33 F4
Romford Pl 46 D4
Romney Av 18 C3
Romsey Clo 33 G3
Ronald St 39 F6
Ronaldsway Dri 29 E1
Ronson Av 36 B3
Rookery Av 38 C6
Rookery La 36 C4
Rope St 30 A3
Rose St 22 A4
Roseacre 29 E5
Roseacre Gro 46 A5
Roseacre La 50 D3
Rosebery St 8 C5
Rosedale Av 19 E2
Rosehill Clo 17 E5
Roseland Cres 17 E5
Rosemary Pl 22 A1
Roseneath Pl 17 E5
Rosetree Av 36 B5
Rosevale Ct 12 C6
Rosevale Rd 12 D6
Rosevale St 17 E5
Rosevean Clo 21 F4
Rosewood Av 17 F1
Ross Clo 40 B3
Rossall Av 34 D3
Rosslyn Rd 39 F5
Rosy Bank 17 F2
Rothbury St 39 F5
Rother Walk 15 E1
Rothesay Av 28 D5
Rothesay Ct 28 D5
Rothesay Rd 39 G6
Rothley Grn 44 B3
Rothsay Av 16 A6
Rothwell St 36 D1
Rotterdam Rd 28 D3
Roughcote La 41 E1
Roundfields 17 F2
Roundway 38 A5
Roundwell St 14 A2
Rowan Dale 39 G2
Rowan Gro 38 A5
Rowan Pl 12 C5
Rowhurst Clo 18 B2
Rowhurst Pl 9 F6
Rowland St 45 E1
Rowley Av 18 D1
Rownall Pl 40 C6
Rownall Rd, Meir 40 C6
Rownall Rd, Werrington 25 F4
Roxburghe Av 39 F6
Royal St 38 D2
Royden Av 22 B5
Roylance St 14 A2
Royston Walk 39 F4
Royville Pl 15 H5
Rubian St 38 B1
Rudyard Gro 19 H5
Rugby Clo 34 D3
Rugby Dri 45 E2
Runnymead Clo 22 D6
Rushcliffe Dri 46 C4
Rushmoor Gro 46 D4
Rushton Clo 11 E3
Rushton Gro 21 E2
Rushton Rd 21 E2
Rushton Vw 50 E2
Rusper Clo 22 C2
Russel Grn 24 D4
Russell St, Dimsdale 19 H4
Russell St, Dresden 45 E1
Russet Gro 8 C2
Rustington Av 39 H4
Ruston Av 9 F5
Rutherford Av 35 F5
Rutherford Pl 30 B5
Rutland Pl 35 H3
Rutland Rd 39 E3
Rutland St 21 E4
Ruxley Ct 22 C6
Ruxley Rd 22 C6
Rycroft Rd 16 A2
Rydal Way 35 F3
Ryder Rd 46 B2
Rye Bank 29 G3
Rye Bank Cres 29 G3
Ryebrook Gro 8 C4
Ryecroft 29 F3
Rylestone Clo 46 D4

Sackville St 30 B2
St Aidens St 14 A1
St Andrews Cres 21 H1
St Andrews Dri 28 D4
St Andrews Sq 31 E5
St Ann St 21 H5
St Annes Vale 10 D1
St Bartholomew Clo 16 B1
St Bernard Pl 22 D4
St Bernards Rd 28 D1
St Chads Rd 14 C2
St Christopher Av 30 B6
St Clair St 39 F6
St Edmunds Av 20 A2
St Georges Av, Bank Top 15 E1
St Georges Av, Dimsdale 19 G4
St Georges Av, Endon 11 H4
St Georges Av Nth 19 G4
St Georges Av West 19 G4
St Georges Cres 42 D1
St Georges Rd 29 E4
St Giles Rd 28 D2
St Gregorys Rd 38 D5
St Helier Clo 34 D4
St James Pl 42 D1
St James St 21 F6
St John St 21 H4
St Johns Av, May Bank 19 H5
St Johns Av, Trent Vale 36 B4
St Johns Pl 28 D1
St Lucys Dri 19 G2
St Luke St 21 H6
St Lukes Clo 27 G2
St Margarets Ct 20 A4
St Margarets Dri 16 A6
St Margarets Gro 38 B5
St Marks Clo 31 F1
St Marks St 31 F1
St Martins La 39 E4
St Martins Rd 29 E4
St Marys Dri 29 E4
St Marys Rd, Sandford Hill 39 G2
St Marys Rd, Wolstanton 20 A3
St Matthew St 38 C1
St Michaels Rd, Cross Heath 29 F1
St Michaels Rd, Little Chell 8 C5
St Nicholas Av 10 A6
St Patricks Dri 28 D4
St Pauls Rd 29 E3
St Pauls St 14 B6
St Peters Walk 21 E2
St Thomas Pl 30 D6
St Vincent Pl 28 D2
Salcombe Pl 21 H1
Salem St 30 D1
Salisbury Av 31 F2
Salisbury St 14 B1
Salkeld Pl 9 F6
Salop Gro 35 H3
Salters Clo 24 D5
Salters La 24 D5
Salwood Clo 45 G1
Sampson St 21 F4
Sandara Clo 14 D3
Sandbach Rd 15 F6
Sandcrest Pl 46 A2
Sandcrest Walk 46 A2
Sandford St, Crackley 12 C6
Sandford St, Sandford Hill 39 F2
Sandgate St 39 G5
Sandhurst Av 46 A1
Sandhurst Clo 19 G4
Sandhurst Pl 46 A2
Sandiway Pl 22 B2
Sandon Av 35 F2
Sandon Old Rd 46 B4
Sandon Rd 46 B3
Sandown Pl 17 E3
Sandown St 21 E6
Sandringham Cres 42 D1
Sandwell Pl 45 H2
Sandwick Cres 22 C3
Sandwood Cres 39 F2
Sandy Hill 25 E4
Sandy La, Baddeley Edge 17 F4
Sandy La, Basford 29 H1
Sandy La, Jobs Pool 11 E2
Sandyfield Rd 22 A4
Sangster La 15 H4
Sant St 14 B6
Saracen Way 46 C1
Sargeant Av 8 D4
Sark Clo 34 C3
Saturn Rd 15 G4
Saunders Rd 19 F5
Scarratt Clo 50 F2
Scarratt Dri 50 F2.
*Scarlett St, Market La 29 G4
Sceptre St 21 F6
School La, Blurton 44 C2
School La, Cookshill 41 F4
School Rd 22 D4
School St, Beasley 18 D2
School St, Newcastle 29 G3
School St, Trent Vale 36 C4
Scot Hay Rd 26 D1
Scotia La 14 C3
Scotia Rd 14 B2
Scott Lidgett Rd 14 A6
Scott Rd 8 D6
Scragg St 8 C1
Scrimshaw Dri 15 F2
Scrivener Rd 30 C2
Seabridge La 34 C3
Seabridge Rd 29 F6
Seaford St 31 F3
Seagrave Pl 35 E1
Seagrave St 29 H3
Seaton Clo 46 A3
Sebring Av 45 H2
Second Av, Porthill 19 G1
Second Av, Townsend 23 H6
Sedbergh Clo 34 D3
Seddon Rd 46 A2
Sedgley Walk 39 F4
Seedfields Rd 38 A4
Sefton Av 22 A1
Sefton Rd 39 H6
Sefton St 21 E6
Selbourne Dri 8 C3
Selby Clo 35 E2
Selby St 40 D2
Selworthy Rd 10 C5
Selwyn St 37 F1
Settle Gro 46 C3
Seven Arches Way 31 G5
Sevenoaks Gro 46 D5
Severn Dri 35 F4